My Child Has Autism,
Now What?

of related interest

Coach Yourself Through the Autism Spectrum
Ruth Knott Schroeder
Foreword by Linda Miller
ISBN 978 1 84905 801 8

Asperger Syndrome After the Diagnosis
7-volume set
Josie Santomauro
Illustrated by Illustrated by Carla Marino

Hints and Tips for Helping Children with Autism Spectrum Disorders
Useful Strategies for Home, School, and the Community
Dion E. Betts and Nancy J. Patrick
ISBN 978 1 84310 896 2

Building a Joyful Life with your Child who has Special Needs
Nancy J. Whiteman and Linda Roan-Yager
ISBN 978 1 84310 841 2

My Child Has Autism, Now What?

10 steps to Get You started

Susan Larson Kidd

Jessica Kingsley *Publishers*
London and Philadelphia

Pictograms reproduced with permission from Martijn van der Kooij

Disclaimer
The information in this book is not intended for use of medical, diagnostic, or other forms of treatment, and the author encourages individuals to seek medical advice and related treatment as needed. Neither the author nor the publisher of this text is responsible for the misuse of information taken in this book.

First published in 2011
by Jessica Kingsley Publishers
116 Pentonville Road
London N1 9JB, UK
and
400 Market Street, Suite 400
Philadelphia, PA 19106, USA
www.jkp.com

Library of Congress Cataloging in Publication Data
A CIP catalog record for this book is available from the Library of Congress

British Library Cataloguing in Publication Data
A CIP catalogue record for this book is available from the British Library

ISBN 978 1 84905 841 4

Printed and bound in Great Britain by
MPG Books Group

To Jeffrey and Sharon

———

thanks for all you have taught me;
you are near and dear to my heart.

Acknowledgments

This book was developed in my head over my 25 years of practice with children with autism and their families. To all of them, I am eternally grateful for teaching me how to connect with, educate, engage, and improve the quality of life for kids.

My sincerest thankfulness goes to my parents, siblings, nieces, and nephews. Thank you for putting up with my ever-whirling brain all these years, which of course leads to a never-quiet mouth!

I could not offer up this work if it weren't for the friendship and support of Elizabeth, Tahirih, Terrie, Sandy, and Kay. You each give me so many unique gifts, all of which contribute to making me a better practitioner and person. Thank you.

Thanks go to Christi Karenget for allowing me to photograph her beautiful children. Love you, Lexi and Bryce!

Gratitude to Martijn van der Kooij for creation and use of PECS for All and Picto Selector. What a great service you have offered to parents worldwide!

I am also grateful to Sandy for being such a good and structured parent that I could access photos in her home on a whim!

Most of all, I thank my husband, Rob, for his encouragement, patience, business sense, and love.

Contents

Introduction:

Beginning the Path

Researching and reading on the internet is a great way to learn about all the options for your newly diagnosed child, but it is often hugely overwhelming. If your child has just been diagnosed with autism and you type "autism" into any common search engine, you will get somewhere around 25,000,000 results from which to begin. Parents tell me that they need a resource at this stage to help empower them to assist their child. Most parents feel terrified at diagnosis and say that the child's whole life passes before their eyes. This causes much anxiety and is debilitating instead of helpful. The parents then seek out resources and are often put on a waiting list, sent loads of paperwork, and/or led down a road they may not truly understand or desire.

Parents ask me to tell them where to start while they wait for other pieces to get into place, and to explain the reason why they are doing a specific intervention. They state that this helps decrease their anxiety and empowers them to take time to make educated decisions about which options are the next best choice for their child.

Parents also tell me that getting started this way helps their overall family dynamics in immeasurable ways and assists them in getting started down a road of progress for their child, instead of waiting and wasting precious time. I hope this book will help you in the same way.

> "The best thing a parent of a newly diagnosed child can do is to watch their child, without preconceived notions and judgments, and learn how the child functions, acts, and reacts to his or her world. That information will be invaluable in finding an intervention method that will be a good match to the child's learning style and needs." (Grandin 2008, p.5)

Do you like rollercoasters?

I like to explain to parents and teachers that raising children with autism can be like a long rollercoaster ride. On a rollercoaster, you go up and down, around and around, fast and slow, and even upside down. If you stay seated, you go that way again and again! Progress with autism is much like this ride: a child will seemingly move forward slowly at times and quickly at other times. A child will make progress up toward a goal, and then go back down, returning to some old behaviors. When something new is learned, some other less desirable behavior may appear. Sometimes something will happen with your child with autism spectrum disorder (ASD) that turns your life upside down. This is very common for kids on the spectrum and helps one to understand that the child isn't necessarily backsliding or retreating into his autism.

In fact, when a child seems to "regress" (that is to say he is doing behaviors we thought he had grown out of or learned to stop) and an old behavior comes back again, it can be a good sign! It may mean that he is learning something new, possibly adapting to a new change in his world, and he regresses to help his brain make the new changes. Like the rollercoaster, as the child's behavior creeps up or zooms down, he is always *still moving forward.* I think the rollercoaster concept helps parents and teachers to appreciate that challenges come and go, that there will be harder times to get through, and rewarding times to celebrate.

So, where to start?

This book is structured to give you—parents, family members, and teachers—enough information to begin any of the suggested steps or interventions without having to research more. It is also written in a pick-up-and-use-immediately fashion, intentionally leaving out the technicalities that often confuse and bury parents. This is done not because you can't handle the jargon, but because right now you don't have time or energy to spend learning the jargon in order to help your child and yourself. Resources for you to learn more are provided for when you have time to look into them further. Also provided are some visuals and examples just to guide you. You don't have to recreate them exactly as it may not be appropriate for your child at the time. As you begin, there are a few basic things to keep in mind.

Rules of thumb to live by

I know that there is a lot to learn, but here are my rules of thumb to guide you:

1. If something doesn't work, try something else.

2. The only expert in autism is a person with autism.

3. Every child with autism is different—what works for one may not work for another.

4. You may not know autism, but you know your child and that is enough.

Number one simply encourages you to keep trying and not get defeated. I have learned that if I keep trying, I will find the right strategy, program, or intervention to help every child somehow. It isn't always easy and frustration does happen, but that is okay—it is to be expected.

Number two is to help you filter out all of the "experts" in the field of autism. What makes someone an expert? Is the experience of one person in one area of autism really enough to call themselves an expert? Which expert do you and your child need? I found early in my work with children and youth on the spectrum that the true expert is *the person with autism spectrum disorder*. Their insight is one you can always trust. Others' information may very well be useful and helpful—indeed, you will benefit greatly from others' work and research in the field—but "expert" status doesn't always mean their work is the only way to go or even particularly right for your child. Keep your filter from your child's perspective and you will make better choices.

Number three is really about understanding how variable autism truly is. Sometimes parents say to me, "So and so is trying that and they say it works wonders for their child." That may be true, but children with autism are so different that it may not also work in your child's case. And that is okay—it is also to be expected. That doesn't mean you don't want to try a highly recommended strategy, program, or therapist; just don't put all your eggs in one basket until you have had time to see what works with and for your child.

1. If something doesn't work, try something else.

2. The only expert in autism is a person with autism.

3. Every child with autism is different—what works for one may not work for another.

4. You may not know autism, but you know your child and that is enough.

Number four—*you may not know autism, but you know your child and that is enough*—is to reveal to you and remind you over and over again that your knowledge and instincts about your own child are solid, helpful, and very important! If you ever feel that you are being disregarded, try again in another way, go someplace else, or get help to be heard. Just because you may be new to autism when sitting among several autism professionals doesn't mean your sense of what is right for your child is inappropriate. You do have a lot to learn, but so do the professionals. I learn more about autism every single day and I have been in this field for over 25 years. We will learn more about your child specifically from you as well.

As a matter of fact, parents have a greater impact on their child's development than any known professional. If parents spend, as a low estimate, just two hours of time interacting with their child daily, they will influence their child's progress two to three times more than any teacher or therapist (Mahoney and McDonald 2007). That is great influence!

What to expect in this book

This is not a book in which you will read about why autism is so prevalent, the theories behind the causes of autism, or explanations of the many programs offered in our world for kids on the spectrum. This book is a book of action. The following steps are in order of what I would consider easiest to hardest to implement based on the amount of time and energy required, and what may help your sanity; but you don't have to do them in this order. I say "what may help your sanity" because sometimes you just have to start with the behavior that drives you crazy! That is okay!

Each step starts off with "why" addressing that issue is helpful. This is to provide you with an explanation of the need to move forward in this area and how it will help your child. Next you will find the "what" and "how" to do. Often I provide you with visual examples of this part of each step along with step-by-step instructions and needed resources. The "when" in each step refers to when to initiate a strategy, how long to try it, or when during the day it is most appropriate to implement. The last section of each step provides you with an opportunity to learn more if you would like to, or for later when you are ready. Take a step a week, a month, or whatever works for you. It is never too late to try, and every attempt helps you learn something useful. Keep in mind that seemingly the only wrong way to approach autism is to not try anything.

Step One:

Help Your Child with Sleeping, Eating, and Toileting

Why?

Many young children with ASD have differences in sensations within their bodies, and, therefore, they may not learn toileting the same way as other children do. These sensory processing differences may also lead the child to be a finicky eater, and not want to go pee or poo-poo in the potty. This is typically very stressful for families and often the first behavior they want help addressing. Additionally, due to similar differences in the brains of children with ASD, they don't often sleep through the night, fall asleep easily, or sleep well. This causes concern for supervision as well as for maturation for the child. Lack of sleep can lead to further difficulties in brain processing and encourage increased crabbiness from your child! Many of you parents then also have difficulty sleeping and this diminishes your capacity to do your best and to be well.

The suggestions below help children on the spectrum with these issues because they address sensory integration dysfunction while applying brain-based strategies to each situation. Communication and structure are also included as components for successful strategies.

SLEEPiNG

What and how?

Wear the child out with physical play 90 minutes or two hours before bedtime. Play vigorously for 30 minutes and do some roughhousing, jumping, or running, if possible. Then provide 30 minutes for cool-down time. Cool-down time can include some independent play or rocking together in a chair, reading, or listening to music. Then create a routine you can stick to while preparing for bedtime with photos or symbols. Routines help the brain retrain itself to get ready for recurring daily events (Duboc 2009; Sonnentag 2006).

Here is how you introduce and teach a bedtime routine.

1. Try to begin at the *same time* each evening with the phrase you want to use to cue the routine such as "Time for bed". The goal is that eventually your child will be able to do the routine independently when you use the cuing phrase.

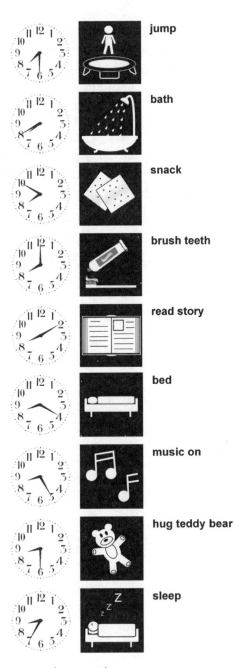

jump

bath

snack

brush teeth

read story

bed

music on

hug teddy bear

sleep

Sleep routine symbols (www.autiplan.com)

2. Place a visual schedule of photos or pictures in the bathroom or bedroom. Use a phrase such as "Check schedule" and point to the top picture. This phrase is functional for use later in life.

3. Prompt the child through each step by saying "What's first?" and then "What's next?" when initially teaching the use of the visual routine schedule. Later, you will want to fade using these prompts so the child does the whole routine independently.

4. Have the child put each visual in the "All done" envelope when she has completed the task. You may have to prompt this at first while teaching the routine as well. For example:

    Parent: Point to photo of toothbrush, say "What's next?"

    Child: Child either says "Brush teeth" or grabs her toothbrush to indicate comprehension of next step.

    Parent: Help child brush teeth as much as necessary, then say "Good job, brushing teeth, all done". Point to tooth brush photo again.

    Child: Takes photo of tooth brush off schedule, inserts into the "All done" envelope.

5. Have the child put the "sleep" visual in the "All done" envelope when she arises first thing in the morning. This helps to teach a complete cycle.

6. Don't "reload" the visual schedule in front of the child; try to do it when she is not around and have it ready by bedtime each evening.

Pajamas on

Brush teeth

Drink water

Go potty

Read story

Time for bed

sleep routine photographs

Sleep routine suggestions

Put on calming music ten minutes before targeted bedtime every night; use the same music daily while establishing this practice. Try to do this on the same schedule for 30 days. I recommend starting with the album *Autumn* or *Summer* by George Winston. Some parents find success with white noise, repetitive environmental sounds, or the consistent sound of a fan. Don't give up until you find what is relaxing for your child! If you choose music, only play the selection for 10–20 minutes so as to not wake the child after she has fallen asleep.

Then go through your bedtime routine of visuals and self-help tasks. Put the child in her bed and try placing a heavy blanket, several blankets, or many pillows over the child while she falls asleep. This type of deep pressure often helps little children with ASD to feel secure in their bed and decreases their anxiety. If your child is one who falls to sleep on her own, but then wakes up in a few hours, try placing the weighted item(s) on the child just after she has fallen asleep. This will often help the child stay asleep longer. You may need to regulate the temperature in the room in order to facilitate the use of heavy blankets. Sleeping more than seven hours a night is crucial for your child to learn, and to be able to regulate her behavior every day. Physicians recommend at least eight hours and up to ten hours of sleep nightly for children (Amen 2005).

Most smells are alerting in nature and may actually keep you awake, especially when the scents are new to you. However, there are some scents that are known to calm the senses, such as lavender, vanilla, ginger, or chamomile. Since one of the easiest ways to scent a room is through candles, and burning candles in a child's room is a fire hazard, place a candle in its jar or votive on a warmer instead. The warmers are electric and warm up the candle enough to disperse the scent throughout the room. You can also find linen sprays or essential oils in these scents. I would recommend introducing a calming scent after establishing the bedtime routine and when it is running fairly smoothly. Otherwise, you might overpower the child's sensory system, and that would be unproductive. When you feel it is time, try the same scent in the bedroom at sleeping time every night for a week or two to test its effects. Only leave the candle warmer on for ten minutes. If using spray, start with just one or two sprays. It has been written that many children with ASD are three times as sensitive to smell as we are. Therefore, we need to barely scent the room. If the smell is offensive to the child, you may be able to tell by the child's increasing activity in a way you haven't seen recently. Scents become calming in the brain when they are familiar, so using a scent consistently at the same time each night may help your child's natural calming process.

If trying routines, music, heavy blankets, and scents doesn't work, consider learning about sleep supplements (see the *To learn more* section below) that help children with ASD (and others!) sleep better and have few to no side effects.

When?

As sleep affects all other areas of a child's processing, trying to get a child to sleep for a good 8–10 hours nightly is really imperative. The sooner you begin to help facilitate this, the better for your child and for you. Also, darkness provides us with our natural sleep hormone so keep that in mind when deciding your child's nightly bedtime as you may need to darken the room if still daylight outside.

If you can't stay on this schedule every day—that is okay! Realistically, with the best intentions, there will be days when you cannot do a routine or schedule. These real-life events can be learning opportunities to help your child learn flexibility. Get back to the routine or schedule as soon as possible, because this regularity and predictability is what your child needs now when they are young in order to learn to be okay with changes over time. Don't beat yourself up when you miss a routine or schedule—life is too short to waste your energy that way! Refocus it on getting back on track.

To learn more

- Supplements that help induce sleep naturally include 5-HTP, valerian root, melatonin, and others. Some of these are made by the body naturally. They typically have no side effects and are not medications. Supplements often help our bodies to make more of what we are lacking. To learn more about this, visit Dr. Amen's website: www.amenclinics.com.

- There is also evidence from thousands of parents of children with ASD that supplements help; to see this, go to: www.autism.com and click on the "Families" link. This will provide you with the "Parent Ratings: Biomedical for Autism" link on the left. There is also a "Parent Ratings: Biomedical for Asperger Syndrome" link.

- If your child takes a prescription medication of any kind, consult your physician before trying any supplements!

- For white noise options, try: www.babywhitenoise.com.

- To generate visuals like the one used on page 17, you can use symbols for free from a wonderful system created by a parent of a child with autism; go to: www.PECSforall.com or www.autiplan.com.

- You can locate a naturopathic doctor, chiropractor, or a DAN physician to help you with supplements for sleeping, along with other biomedical strategies when you are ready. See the *To learn more* section of *Step Nine* for these resources.

- To learn more about prompting and fading prompts, type those terms into an internet search engine, or try: www.bbbautism.com/prompting_and_fading.htm.

EATING

What and how?

First, provide your child the opportunity to jump, swing, or rock—whichever is calming to her—for ten minutes before sitting down to eat. Start the mealtime session with calming music—the same music at the same time daily. Calming music naturally lowers blood pressure and stress, therefore allowing your child an opportunity to focus on the food. Many children with ASD are finicky eaters because of sensory processing differences. They may not like foods with strong odors or with slimy textures or strong tastes; or they may only like one or two specific foods. Helping the child with these calming procedures first may help her to tolerate more foods or a variety of foods better.

To have an older child stay seated at the table for eating, try a weighted vest. This provides some deep pressure that may help her feel more comfortable while seated. Put the vest on right before sitting down to eat. Take it off right after the eating session, or after ten minutes. Also, to help keep a child seated at the table, you can use a visual such as two photos, one of the table setting and one of some rewarding activity the child likes to do. Then you show the photos and say "First eat, then *train*." Place the visuals on the table so the child can refer back to them as needed or so you can use them as a prompt for a reminder.

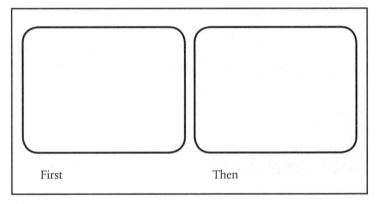

"First, then" sample format

It is important to insist gently that children try a variety of foods. If kids don't try to expand their food tolerance and food preferences, they might not eat healthily across their lifespan. It is much harder to teach them this when they get older, so it is better to try when the children are young. You don't have to try this strategy at every meal every day! You can pick just lunch, or just dinner, and try these suggestions. When you see your child eating better and tolerating more foods, then you can expand the strategies to another mealtime.

Eating routine suggestions

To encourage a child to eat more foods, use Grandma's Principle: "First you eat your peas, then you get your dessert". Prepare the food you know the child likes: for example purposes, let's say a grilled cheese sandwich. Cut the sandwich into small bite-size pieces and keep them on a plate close to you. Then prepare something you want the child to eat: let's say vegetables. Try raw vegetables because they are crunchy and less smelly; crunchy and less odorous foods are generally more tolerable. Then you say "One bite carrot, then sandwich". Only give the child one small piece of the sandwich at a time. The child will likely not cooperate at first, but if you remain strong and consistent, the child will do what you ask because she is hungry. You can also try graduated steps toward eating on the first few days such as "Touch the carrot", "Smell the carrot", "Kiss the carrot", "Lick the carrot", then "One bite", etc. Model the action for your child as you say it. This strategy helps to shape a child's behavior with little steps toward your main goal of eating the carrot, or whatever food you are introducing.

First eat   Then train

"First eat, then train"

Most parents are very worried that if they try such strategies, their child will go hungry, but that simply isn't so. There will be some foods the child never likes, just like the rest of us, but if you don't try this behavioral strategy, the child's long-term health may be compromised by eating only a limited selection of foods. As mentioned above, this could be detrimental as she will not get the nutrition she needs. The sooner you work with your child to try a variety of foods, the easier it will be for her to learn to desensitize to the textures, odors, or other sensory aspects of food.

It may also help to try to find foods similar to the ones your child likes. For example, if she will eat an apple, but not a banana, try and experiment with more foods similar in texture to the apple—a pear, a jicama, or a firm plum. In addition to teaching your child to try new food, you may want to consider having your child take vitamins. Parents get very resourceful at putting vitamins into foods the child likes—vitamins come in liquid forms to help this process. Supplementing with vitamins helps the child to stay healthier by keeping her immune system stronger while she is learning to eat healthier foods. (See the *To learn more* section below for information on liquid vitamins.)

Another strategy that may help your child eat is to stimulate the child's face and gums with a vibrating toy before eating. There is a special nerve in this area of the face and mouth that responds well to vibration and may help the child tolerate textures and tastes better. Help the child to bite on or hold the toy in her mouth or around her face for ten minutes before eating. She can "play" like this while she is sitting in her chair at the table as you prepare some food. This is a sensory integration strategy and you can find more resources on this in *Step Three*.

When?

As most children eat something, even though it may not be the best for her, tackling eating depends on what else you are working with at the time. Some people want to address this immediately, while others choose something else first. The thing about eating strategies is that you can try one just at one meal a day—it doesn't have to be every meal every day to be effective.

To learn more

- There are some good and easy ideas to help address eating aversions by other parents at the following web address: www.comeunity.com/disability/sensory_integration/resources.html.

- To find liquid vitamins or quality supplements, go to www.iherb.com and type "liquid vitamins" or the supplement name into the site's search function.

- To find face massagers and vibrating toys, go to: www.beyondplay.com/CATALOG/ORA1.HTM.

TOILETING
What and how?

Believe it or not, the book *Everyone Poops* (Gomi 2001) is really helpful here! Even if your child can't process the abstract language, some of the visuals along with the sequence provide the child with a sense that this sensation and process is okay. You can also make your own Social Story™

using photos or drawings of the process of sitting on the toilet, poo poo and pee in the potty, flushing the toilet and everyone being okay with that.

This is the toilet.

The toilet is for pee pee.

Everyone goes pee pee.

When Mommy says "time for pee pee", I go sit on the toilet.

Then I go pee pee in the toilet.

I get to flush the toilet when I am all done!

Then I wash my
hands and dry
my hands.

I went pee pee in the
potty. I did it and I
am happy!

"I go pee pee in the potty"—Social Story™ example. (Social
Stories are a concept developed by Carol Gray.)

I have come to believe that children on the spectrum who
avoid pooping in the toilet do so often because of their
sensory processing. They may not like the smallness of the
bathroom, the sound of the toilet flushing, the sensation of
a bowel movement, and the smell may be overwhelming to
their neural system (more so than to ours!).

Pooping suggestions

Pooping may be such a problem that you have had to
intervene medically. Sometimes, there are issues with the
child's gut that may be contributing to these toileting issues
that you should always address with your doctor. (See *Step
Nine* for more information regarding that.) However, even
if there has been medical intervention, these strategies may
help the sensory and behavioral issues around toileting.

1. First, put a calming scented diffuser of some kind in your bathroom—I suggest trying lavender as it seems accepted by many kids. It is important not to offend the child's smelling system, so only set it up for a few minutes prior to the child going into the bathroom, or spray a slight amount, as children's sense of smell is developmentally much more accurate than ours. Use organic essential oils if possible to avoid allergy issues.

2. Secondly, before asking the child to sit in the bathroom, open a window to help with potential overstimulation of smell issues. If you don't have a window, place a fan away from the child but in the direction to move air out of the bathroom. Sometimes having time with the fan in another room first may help to be sure your child is not offended in a sensory way by the movement or sound of the fan.

3. Third, using pictures or a Social Story, review twice daily with your child that she is going to poop in the toilet. We have done this at school as well and found that to be very helpful.

4. Fourth, gradually lead your child into the bathroom, and encourage her with a small reinforcer. For this to work, you must choose one of the child's favorite treats, and only give this reinforcer when successfully going into the bathroom, staying in the bathroom, and going potty in the toilet. If the reinforcer is to stay powerful, you can't allow the child to have it at any other time during the toilet training time window! I choose a particular favorite treat for this and only give one piece when reinforcing. This is to encourage the child to want to experience the discomfort to earn the treat. This is what many people refer to as helping the child gently to desensitize to something. I and many families have had

good success with Skittles, cheesy crackers (e.g. Goldfish), M&Ms, or sugar free Gummy-Bears.

Here is an example of how you may shape your child's behavior. Show a visual story of pooping. Walk your child to the bathroom, say "Go poo poo in the potty" or whatever you want to be your cuing phrase. Then give your child one small candy (I like Skittles) and praise her. The next day, show the visual story, walk your child to the bathroom, say your cuing phrase, and walk into the bathroom. Then praise your child and give her one of the same small candies. The next day, show the visual story, walk your child to the bathroom, say your cuing phrase, walk into the bathroom, and have the child remove her pants. Then reward with one of the same small candies and praise. Each day, add the next step in the process and reinforce each step along the way. Additional steps may include just sitting briefly on the toilet, sitting on the toilet until the bell timer goes off, sitting and going potty, sitting and going and wiping, then add flushing, "You did it", pants on, and wash hands!

5. Fifth, you must take time with the child to sit on the toilet and keep her there long enough to relax and go to the toilet. So, have a set of books and a bucket full of fidgets that are for play while on the toilet in the bathroom, along with some songs and even some potty songs (see *To learn more* below). I recommend taking your young child to the bathroom every 30 minutes while teaching this. If school folks are helping to teach toileting at the same time, they will want to use the 30-minute schedule as well.

Happy bucket for toileting

6. Sixth, you may also need to teach the wiping, flushing, and "pants back on" aspects of this process along with washing hands. I would use visuals for these too. Be sure to praise the child for having dry pull-ups, diaper, or underwear too. We want to teach her what "dry" means.

7. Calming music—music that is 60 beats per minute or less—can be on in the background for ten minutes while you are working on this with your child. Music such as this helps our bodies to calm in a natural way without effort, so this can always be helpful. Sometimes, we use songs with motions that we sing while the child is on the potty, and we let the child choose them from some visual cues. (There are more ideas about music use in *Step Five*.)

pants down

sit on toilet

wash hands

dry hands

Toileting routine

When?

Toileting issues likely need to be addressed soon, especially if you have had to give your child laxatives or enemas to help them with this. Remember, you don't have to tackle all steps of this at once, just one step at a time or as many as seems practical for you to be successful. Starting with peeing in the potty is usually a good first step.

To learn more

- Using story books helps children on the spectrum to understand the whole process of what may and may not happen. Please go to www.carnegielibrary.org, select the "Kids" link, type "toilet training" into the search box, and several book lists will appear. Or, type "toilet training kids' books" into any search engine.

- A cute potty song by *Blues Clues*: www.nickjr.com/printables/blues-toilet-song.jhtml.

- Also, fun and distracting songs from *Wee Sing Silly Songs* are great. These are widely available from Amazon and elsewhere.

- For more intensive toileting programming, see Chapter 10 of *Self-Help Skills for People with Autism* by Anderson, Jablonski, Thomeer and Knapp (2007) Woodbine House.

- Social Stories (e.g. pages 28–30) are very helpful for eating, sleeping, and toileting issues, and will be helpful for you to use with your child for years to come in many other ways. To get started, see Carol Gray's website: www.thegraycenter.org.

- For natural aromatherapy selections, go to: www.escentsaromatherapy.com.

Step Two:
Help Your Child by Using Visual Supports

Why?

Most children on the spectrum have difficulties communicating. The children may not use words, they may use some words or gestures, they may respond to some verbal requests but not many, they may seem to ignore you, they may get frustrated when trying to ask for something they want, or they may use inappropriate behaviors to get their needs met (e.g. when I climb on the furniture, I get Mom's attention and then she will help me get my juice). The term "visual supports" is used to describe items that help children with ASD to communicate more easily and to regulate more readily. Photographs are very concrete—that is, there is very little symbolism needed to interpret a photograph of something. Therefore, pictures are good visual supports to use to communicate with the child, and to help the child communicate with you. Additionally, pictures help the child to know what to expect in his environment while he struggles to interpret all of the incoming stimulation. Photos or pictures are a good foundation to start with before trying to use symbols.

Experts in autism—the people with autism themselves—tell us that they *see* words and *hear* language in pictures in their minds (Freed and Parsons 1997). Temple Grandin tells us that she translates what people say into movies in her mind's eye. This is why starting the use of visual supports with photographs makes so much sense. Even if your child has some words he uses, or you can tell that he understands your language pretty well, it never hurts a child's development to use pictures or other visuals. Using pictures first also helps to ensure you have helped your child to build a solid foundation of understanding some language concepts before you move to more complex language or more abstract communication systems.

In new situations, pictures are very helpful to children with ASD to help decrease their anxiety about the unknown. For example, when a little one with ASD started preschool recently, he began to spend more time jumping and flapping his hands than ever before, according to his mother. He seemed overwhelmed and fatigued daily as well, and didn't seem to want to go to school. His mother and I built him a visual schedule for school along with photos of his teacher, some of his peers, and his school therapists. We used the photos to create a few Social Stories about preschool expectations as well. He began to calm instantly upon implementation of these photographs as visual support.

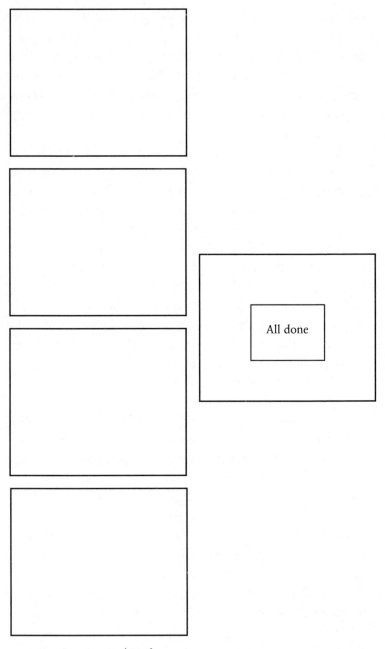

All done

sample visual schedule format

What and how?

Here is how to get started using photographs as visual supports for young children.

1. Get a digital camera and a good color printer. (As your child develops, you will use this printer a lot to make Social Stories, use visual symbols, and use software such as *Communicate: SymWriter* which is a symbol/word software.) Take 10–20 minutes to learn how to connect the camera to your computer and how to download pictures into a photo program. It helps when two people in the family can learn to do this. Older siblings are a great resource for this too.

2. Next, take pictures of the most common areas the child is in around your home—his bedroom, the bathroom he uses, the kitchen table where you have him sit to eat, the play area, the back yard. Also take a photo of your vehicle or the vehicle the child travels in. Photos are the most concrete visual we can use (next to an actual article, such as a cracker exchanged for a cracker). Even some kids who have some words still benefit from using photographs before using picture symbols.

3. Next, take a picture of the most common objects your child needs or wants, such as a juice box he likes, the cereal he likes, the toy or blanket he prefers, the cup he drinks from, the toilet, the bathtub, his bed. When taking these photos, be careful to zoom in as much as possible and eliminate other distractions from the photo. For example, I place the cup or toy right on the table with nothing else on it, and then take the photo from above the item. This way, we are communicating only the single item in the photo to the child, and we are being clear with him what we are talking about.

Drink

Cracker

Toy

simple photos of a child's favorite items

Another example to highlight the importance of the clarity of the photo is this: if you take a picture of your car and it is in front of the garage in the photo, when you say "car", are you teaching your child about the car, the garage, or both? This can cause confusion to the child and may lead to stimulus overselectivity. (You don't need to know all about this right now in order to proceed, but you can read more about it from the *To learn more* list at the end of this section.)

This photo does show the car, but also another vehicle and the garage.

This photo is a clearer example of "car" because there are no other vehicles or places visible next to it.

4. Also, take a happy head and shoulders shot of the people in the house, family, and anyone else who cares for the child.

5. Print the photos. When printing the photos, make them 5 x 3 inches or 6 x 4 inches. This way, you can glue them to an index card if you want to make them sturdier. Print three copies of each to start with.

6. Take one set of the object photos and place them in a convenient and accessible location for the child—

the refrigerator or the bedroom mirror, for example. I would start with the juice box, cup, and favorite snack. When you think your child wants one of these items, go to the refrigerator and pull off the photo. Using simple language, say "I want juice" while handing the picture to the child. Then take the picture from the child and say "Okay, Tommy wants juice" and get the juice for him. Put the photo back in its location on the refrigerator. The goal is for the child to make the connection that this photo handed to Mom helps me to get what I want. It empowers the child with communication intent. It also will help the child to understand that this is one way he can communicate his needs and wants with others in his environment. Again, even if the child is using some words or phrases, the visual helps to clarify the power of communication and language use.

7. Having the photographs accessible to the children is imperative so that they can communicate with you when they need to. This is why we should make them easy to transport. To make a "go with you" card ring or system, take five of the most commonly requested photos and place them on index cards and hole punch them at the top. Then place them on a one-inch book ring, commonly found at an office store, along with the clips from lanyards. Then you can clip the ring to the child's pants or belt loop, or place it on a chain around his neck if it is safe to do so.

8. When the child asks you for a drink by pulling you to the sink, for example, locate the drink photo on the card ring, say "Drink" while pointing to it and then get the drink. This way you are teaching the child to use the pictures to request items as well as teaching the language concept that this photo represents (the word "drink"). I

typically start with these five photo cards on the ring: "drink", "potty", "cracker" or "cookie" (whichever one the child is likely to request most frequently), a favorite toy, and "Mommy" or the main daily caregiver. Just as with the drink, when the child becomes upset, you can point to the "Mommy" photo, say "Mommy, help" and then comfort the child. Again, you are teaching him to initiate communication in a concrete way.

"Go with you" visual example   "Use your pictures"

9. Keep an envelope of pictures most commonly served for breakfast, lunch, or dinner near the dining table. This way you have them at your fingertips and can encourage your child to communicate by asking for more of the items or choosing between two food choices.

10. To use the photographs during a meal, select two photos of menu choices—for example macaroni and chicken. Place the two photos in child's sight, but out of his reach. Then point to the macaroni photo and say "Macaroni". Put a small amount of macaroni on the child's plate. When you can see they are ready for more, place the photos within reach and help the child choose

the macaroni photo and push it towards you. You say "More macaroni, please" or "You want more macaroni." This way you are teaching the child to use the photo to request, as well as the words and phrases they can eventually use to request later on.

When?

Using photographs and other visual cues really helps children to be less anxious and to communicate more quickly. If you can only start with a few, that is a good start. The more you add, the more you will find helpful for your child. Additionally, this may help deter the development of inappropriate behaviors to get the child's needs met—such as biting or pinching—when he has a visual system that helps him to communicate.

Here is a tip for you as your child grows older and becomes more verbal or more communicative: don't stop using visuals! When children on the spectrum become upset, they can't use their language and other skills as easily, and they continue to rely on visuals to help them regulate. Furthermore, as children become more successful with words, parents and teachers often think a child doesn't need the visuals anymore—but they do! Just modify the visuals to the new level of the child by using symbols and then by adding words, and eventually only using words.

To learn more

- For an awesome symbol system that is easy to use and free, go to: www.pecsforall.com.

- There are many more layers of visual supports to learn about when you are ready. It can get complicated and overwhelming, so take small chunks at a time. One book I think can be helpful when you are ready to move on is *Visual Strategies for Improving Communication* by Linda A. Hodgdon (1995), published by QuirkRoberts Publishing.

- *Thinking in Pictures* by Temple Grandin (1995/2006), published by Random House. This book from an adult with autism helps us to understand how very visual people with autism can be and how helpful visuals are in processing their world.

- Stimulus overselectivity and other pertinent information can be learned from *Pivotal Response Training* by Koegel, retrievable online by entering "Pivotal Response Training" into an internet search engine.

- Eventually, you may want to purchase *Boardmaker* for symbol creation and use from Mayer-Johnson, Inc. *Communicate: SymWriter* is also a Mayer-Johnson product. See: www.mayer-johnson.com.

- Later on, you may be interested in learning the official Picture Exchange Communication System (PECS). See: http://en.wikipedia.org/wiki/Picture_Exchange_Communication_System.

step Three:

Incorporate Sensory integration Strategies

Why?

In *Step One*, I mentioned that most children with ASD have different ways of processing sensations from their environment and in their bodies than many of us do. These brain differences cause sights, sounds, temperatures, pain, pressure, smells, touch, tastes, and movement to feel differently than they feel in and to us. Although simplified here, this is called sensory integration dysfunction. Other terms for similar conditions include sensory integration disorder, sensory processing disorder, or sensory processing dysfunction.

Children with ASD behave uniquely in different settings and to different stimulation than other children do (Grandin 1995). For example, a sweet young boy that I had the privilege of working with told me that when he was little, he was very afraid of the vacuum cleaner. He explained that when his mom vacuumed in the house, he would run to his bedroom and hide under the covers or in the closet. When asked why he did this, he said he wasn't sure, but he thought it was because the sound hurt his ears. Then he proceeded to tell me this no longer bothers him, because he has grown up (he was ten!). I have worked with many children with autism who are afraid of the vacuum cleaner—this causes much disruption in a household!

Sensory integration dysfunction often causes much anxiety in the child with autism and may be the cause for safety concerns. Many kids will spend every evening exhibiting troublesome behavior because they fear the vacuum is going to come on. This may also be caused by some other noise in a room or a vehicle. Flickering lights (fluorescents) are another common cause of sensory discomfort to children on the spectrum. They may become agitated around them, or anxious that they have to be in the lights (this is quite common in school classrooms where fluorescent lighting is standard). The problem is compounded by the anxiety that sensory processing dysfunction generates and contributes to overloading a child's neurological system. And the child likely cannot explain this to you.

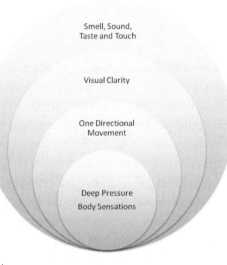

Smell, Sound,
Taste and Touch

Visual Clarity

One Directional
Movement

Deep Pressure
Body Sensations

sensory systems

Sometimes, children with autism don't register pain such as a burn or cut the same way others do, or they don't demonstrate when they feel ill in a typical way or the way we may expect. Therefore, addressing as many sensory issues as possible helps the child to be safe, feel safe, and to regulate in her world more easily. It also helps you to see that your child's behavior stems from inside her special brain, and not because you are not a good parent or some other inadequacy parents might feel when their child responds differently to them. I always like to think that an inappropriate behavior may be telling us that the child needs some help in processing sensory information so that we don't punish her for something she cannot help.

One of the most common parts of sensory dysfunction kids with ASD experience is the craving of deep pressure. This is related to a sensation we mostly take for granted called proprioception. This pushing and pulling sensation in our joints and muscles helps us to discern our body awareness, stay calm, and remain in control of our body in any environment. You can tell children need this when they run around in a small space a lot, body-slam into the wall and furniture, and jump up and down excessively. Some behaviors and tantrums from children are displayed because they have become dysregulated—that is to say they are overwhelmed by too many stimuli or are too confused by the stimuli and they shut down in some way. Some kids shut down because they don't get enough of the input needed to stay regulated.

Although proprioception and other sensory processing is more complicated than this, I want you to be able to provide some help for your child in this area now as it has long and lasting effects. Not all children qualify for sensory integration therapy (therapeutic treatment by a licensed professional) with an occupational therapist. This is another reason why it is important for parents and teachers to be able to implement some of these strategies. You can read and learn more from the resources listed below when you are ready.

What and how?

Here are ten strategies and ideas to get you started in sensory integration with your little one.

1. I have found that a mini trampoline can be the best friend of a parent and teacher of children with ASD! With little ones, you can hold their hands over their heads and help them jump up and down, providing lots of good pressure input. This helps many children to calm down. You can make games out of this jumping time too by practicing the alphabet, counting, or singing songs with your child while she jumps. Try this for 5–10 minutes for every 20–30 minutes you want

your child to attend to something, such as sitting at the table to eat, going through the dressing routine, or sitting on the floor to play together.

Mini trampoline

Beanbags provide deep pressure helping children to sit calmly.

2. Some kids on the autism spectrum don't need calming activity as much as they need help to remain emotionally stable or to focus. Jumping on the mini trampoline can also provide this needed input. Also, activities that naturally provide pushing–pulling input will help your child to regulate sensations. For example, having them push around one of their moving toys with something to weigh it down a bit to provide that input is a natural and fun way for the child to get needed input. Or they can pull the wagon full of their toys around. I have seen some little ones push chairs around the house for this same reason. I encourage them to push the chairs to the table or some other functional action. You can also use some visual cues to make a "road" for your child to push a toy onto. Poly dots or foam squares make good choices

for a "road". See the *To learn more* section below for places to find these items. It seems that, sometimes, a slight physical activity of this nature helps children on the spectrum to calm or regulate emotions and sensation more easily.

Ten-minute rule

When trying a sensory strategy, such as putting a weighted vest on your child, or participating in a sensory activity such as swinging or jumping, only do this for about ten minutes. The average child's brain adapts to sensory changes in 8–11 minutes. Since we don't know how the child with sensory issues is going to respond to a sensory strategy, or because we want the sensory strategy to help the child either to calm or to remain focused, ten minutes is a good amount of time to use as a guideline. Once you get to know how your child responds, then you can adjust the time to more if needed. *Caution:* Don't allow your child to do a sensory activity too much longer than ten minutes even if you see a good response because you don't want the activity to have the opposite effect!

3. Another fun way to provide proprioceptive deep pressure input to your child is to play the sandwich game. You can use beanbag chairs or couch cushions for this. Say "Let's play sandwich" and then lay down a cushion and say "Here's bread". Then have the child lay down next and say "You are the meat". Then put a beanbag on top and say "That's the mustard" and continue in this fashion. You end up with a big pile of cushions and beanbags on top of the child and then you can finish by pretending to take a bite and wrestle the pile with your child in it. As your child learns the game, you can be the

one to be in the sandwich, and you can have your other children play along as well.

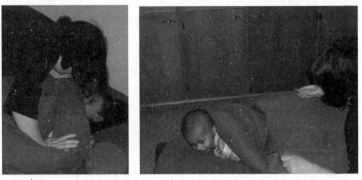

sandwich game

4. If your child continues to jump from furniture or high stairs, they may be craving this proprioceptive input. To replace that, create a safe place for them to jump down into cushions or beanbags. You can buy child-safe plastic stairs to jump from, or use a small stairway in your house by placing the beanbag chairs or couch cushions at the bottom, and visually indicating where the child can jump from (I taped outlines of my feet on the stair the child was allowed to jump from to provide a visual cue).

5. Vestibular input can sometimes be calming for children on the spectrum too. Vestibular input is basically movement. You can tell movement is calming for your child if riding in a car soothes her and she seems to love that. If this is the case, your child may love to swing. Swings are available which you can use inside your home in doorways. These cradle your child, providing some deep pressure and calming motion. As long as the movement is only in one direction and slowly paced,

it may be calming. Swing for small intervals of time remembering and applying the ten-minute rule (see page 51). This will help ensure your child benefits from the swing as calming and not overstimulating.

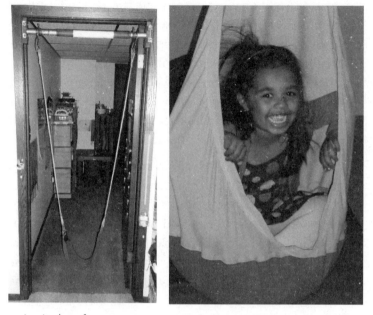

swing in doorframe   swing from IKEA

6. A rocking chair may be another calming place for your child to sit at stressful times throughout the day. If you can hug your little one deeply while rocking her, that may be calming. Putting a heavy blanket on the child in the rocker can also enhance the calming process.

7. Often, little children with ASD go through periods when they don't want to wear their clothes and they prefer to run around the house naked. This sensation is referred to as tactile defensiveness. Although running around with few or no clothes on is okay at some

ages, it is not likely to be okay in most environments as children mature. This therefore requires us to help them learn to wear clothes! Believe it or not, jumping and some vestibular input may help your child leave her clothes on because she can regulate and tolerate clothes better. Additionally, you can cut the tags off clothes, turn them inside out, and rewash them several times to help them become more tolerable. Stick with the same clothes that your little one will tolerate. For example, if she likes a specific brand of pants, get more of those. If she tolerates short sleeve t-shirts with no binding in the sleeves, get more of those. Sweatpants are often tolerated better by little ones than jeans.

8. It is good to teach the rules about when and where to wear clothes early on. I would include some visuals— clothes on at school, clothes off in the bath tub, for instance—to help your child understand the rules. Or create a Social Story about clothes and where we have to wear them and where we can be clothes-free. These steps will help your child stay dressed longer while she learns to desensitize to touch.

Everyone wears clothes. I wear clothes too.

Sometimes, clothes bother me. I still have to wear them.

I have to wear clothes to school.

I have to wear clothes to church.

I have to wear clothes to the store.

I can take off my clothes when I am at home.

I can take off my clothes when I am taking a bath.

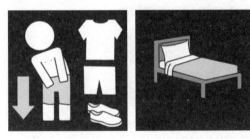

I can take off my clothes when I go to sleep.

I wear my clothes when I have to and I am happy.

social story "I wear my clothes"

9. Choosing from these sensory integration activities periodically throughout the day is what will help your child to regulate her sensations more evenly. So make a plan to implement some jumping times, some swinging times, and some other sensory game times at intervals throughout the day. This will ensure the child doesn't have to become dysregulated in order to get her needs met. See Appendix A for a format and sample of a sensory plan for home and/or school.

10. When children on the spectrum are between the ages of two and six, it is important to allow them some time to "revert back" to self-stimulatory behaviors for a short period of time each day. This means that you allow them to do the activity that is seemingly purposeless to us—such as spinning objects, dropping objects and jumping, or finger-flicking at the ceiling fan. This behavior is really serving a purpose for the child's brain as a way to integrate her responses to her environment, and to decompress from the demands being placed on her. Although we don't want this activity to go on too long each day, five to ten minutes once or twice a day without consequence or interruption may be very helpful to your child. More than this and it becomes unproductive for your child. But as she grows, you will see she requires this unstructured time less and less.

When?

Sensory integration strategies are useful from the first moment you try them. Although not a quick fix by any means, sensory integration (SI) is an area that you will need to continue to learn about as your child grows. I believe sensory dysfunction explains a lot of young children's autistic-like behaviors, and therefore should be addressed as part of a whole-child approach to treatments and intervention. You don't need to know it all now, as it can easily become complicated, so just do what you can. A parent once berated herself to me—she said she only got to do one sensory integration strategy a day with her little boy as she had two other children in the house as well. She felt guilty because she knows her child with ASD needs the sensory integration strategies and she could see how much they helped him. She stated she thought she should be doing them all day long. You know what I told her? I said, "Now your child is getting one sensory strategy every day, when, prior to you doing this with him, he was getting none! Keep it up and add another when you can." Good for her and good for you.

To learn more

- There is a book written in the 1970s by Jean Ayers that is very useful in explaining autism and sensory dysfunction. She was an occupational therapist and the title of the book is *Sensory Integration and the Child* published by Western Psychological Services. It contains a chapter just for parents. You can find this book on eBay and at online bookstores.

- Another very good resource to take you further in sensory integration with your child is a book called *Raising a Sensory Smart Child* by Lindsey Biel and Nancy Peske, two occupational therapists (2005, Penguin Books).

- I suggest reading some chapters of one of these books prior to searching on the internet to help guide you to useful information in this area specific to your child. This will help you discern through all of the information you get when you type "sensory integration" into a search engine on the internet.

- To shop for sensory "stuff" including swings and polydots, you can go to: www.flaghouse.com or www.theraproducts.com.

- For jigglers and other vibrating toys for oral stimulation, see: www.beyondplay.com.

- I also purchase many sensory items at home and garden stores such as Kmart and Target. For mini trampolines, you can purchase online through Amazon or at Target or Walmart.

- To learn how to make your sensory games more interactive, more language-based, or add a sensory hook to your game, go to this website for parents of children with ASD: www.autismgames.org.

- Have your child assessed by an occupational therapist who is experienced with children on the autism spectrum. Some children qualify for occupational therapy to help them with sensory processing. See *Step Eight* for more information on resources for this.

- For cool and unusual sensory toys such as the *Clackerz* pictured on page 40, shop at Play Visions: www. playvisions.com.

- Shop at IKEA for a variety of swings, rockers, and hammocks: www.IKEA.com.

Step Four:
Simplify Areas in Your Home

Why?

Often, homes are overstimulating for children with autism spectrum disorders. There are too many sights, sounds, smells, textures, and people coming and going for a child to process and this causes him distress. This distress may come out in many ways such as isolation, self-stimulatory behaviors, tantrums, meltdowns, frequent crying, or aggressiveness.

Some children's repetitive behaviors may come from their way of organizing. They may do these behaviors to help control overstimulation. For example, some little ones with ASD like to line up their blocks in a certain row, or will only put red blocks with red blocks and get upset if they are mixed up. Sometimes they do this for a visual effect, which is a sensory kind of behavior, but sometimes they are ordering their environment the best way they know how. Therefore, organizing and simplifying even a few areas in your home may help your child to regulate better, and thus be more available for interaction and other daily activities.

These simplifying ideas will also help your child with ASD to visually organize his home and thereby to understand better what behavior should occur in what area. For example, if the blocks are put in a specific spot on the toy cubby or shelf in the play area of a room, then it helps your child to know where they belong when they are not in use, and that the blocks don't belong in the kitchen or hallway.

Simplifying areas in your home further helps provide a safe, calm, and structured place where your child can play and learn. It also helps the environment become predictable for your child which may help decrease anxiety. Typically, children can create this for themselves; however, children with ASD need our help to do so.

How and what?

1. The first step is to reduce overstimulating smells and sights in your home. Eliminate scented plug-ins and scented spray cleansers or air fresheners. Put up dark blinds or shades in the child's bedroom and one play area in the house because different light levels may be offensive to your child's sensory system. Eliminate the television, computer, hand-held electronic games, and most toys that you want to control access to. Choose two or three selected toys to be out in the child's room or play area. Use lamplight instead of fluorescent bulbs as the flickering of fluorescent light is often offensive in a sensory way to children with ASD. If you don't want the child to be distracted by what happens outside,

try not to structure eating, learning, or playing near a window.

2. Eliminating smells in the kitchen and bathroom is often a greater challenge. Using environmentally friendly soaps and cleansers may help, but sometimes food odors dissipate while cooking. If you know your child does not like a certain food, he may avoid the kitchen when you cook that food item, or may try to get away from the smell. Sometimes this is just something we need to teach the child to adjust to. For example, if you cook cabbage for the rest of the family and know that your child with ASD dislikes it very much, just say "That is cabbage, it stinks and I don't like it". You are giving the child the language here to learn to adapt to that smell. Likewise, after an offensive bathroom odor, you can simply say "Peeyou, that is stinky. I don't like it." You can use fans and open windows to help dissipate food smells. The key is to think about smells that we typically adapt to without conscious acknowledgment. This will help you to be more mindful of smells that may offend your little one.

3. To help the child process the coming and going of people which can be disruptive to his routine, use photographs. Take photos of the people in your child's world. In the morning on a day when you expect company, show him that Aunty Susan is coming today by showing him the photograph. You can leave the photo on the refrigerator inside a drawing of your house. This will be a visual reminder of who is coming to visit today. Sometimes, you may have to put several photographs in the "house" on the fridge, and just tell your child who each person is and that they are coming for a visit. You can also do this at school and/or daycare with therapists and other

visitors by placing the photos in the same spot daily. This is an abstract concept, but because you consistently use photographs in the same way for the same behavior (people visiting your home), your child learns this concept in a concrete way.

Example of visual communication of house visitors. Place in a location easy for child to see.

4. Another way to simplify your home is to look at each space and see that it visually represents the function it serves. For example, if you have a television in your kitchen, that visually tells children that TV-watching behavior can occur in the kitchen. What we really want the kitchen to portray is that this is the room we gather together, eat calmly at the table, and communicate with each other. Another example is that the bedroom is for sleeping, not for jumping and playing during the night. Therefore, be sure that play items are put away before bedtime in the toy chest, cubby, or closet, or designate another room or space in your house where play occurs.

Visually clear play space

Visually unclear play space

5. Organizing play items with visuals and labels is a
    strategy that will not only help you to keep organized
    and to remember what materials and toys a child has,
    but it will also teach the child the symbolism of visuals,
    what they communicate, and a useful way to organize
    as he grows. For example, I suggest buying five see-
    through bins with lids. Take a photograph of five
    toys—let's say the blocks, the plastic animals, the balls,
    cars, and the dolls. (Refer to *Step Three* to review how to
    take clean and visually articulate photographs for clear
    communication.) Place the items in the bins, and tape the
    photograph and simple label—such as "BLOCKS"—on
    the front cover. Then you can stack these bins in the
    child's cubby in the play area, or next to the sofa, or in
    the child's closet. When you take the items out for play,
    say "You want the blocks" and point to the cover. When
    play with blocks is finished, help the child to clean
    up and put blocks back into their respective bucket,
    easily designated to the child by the visual. You are
    teaching your child here about communication, about
    being responsible for his belongings, to cooperate in
    clean up, and how to keep things organized. You are
    also teaching him the concepts of matching and sorting,
    which are cognitive skills necessary for reading and
    math development. And, ultimately, you are helping
    your child to learn these things in a calmer, more serene
    surrounding.

Clearly labeled bins

6. You may want to use colors to help organize your child's belongings. You can use green plastic bins for toys, yellow plastic bins for books, and red plastic bins for music things, for example. Colors are a helpful and clear visual organizer, and are known to help the brain remember things more easily. I would still use a photo and simple label for the front of these bins to foster cognitive development.

7. Visual jigs can be used to help simplify an area or space in a functional way for your child. A jig is a visual outline that cues a behavior without having to use any words. For example, you can trace an outline of cup, plate, and spoon on a placemat. Then the child can visually see where each of those items belongs. You can outline the child's shoes on a floor rug by the door. This visually tells the child that is where his shoes belong when he is not wearing them. You can even put a hula hoop on the floor in the family room and teach the child that he needs to stay within that hoop while he plays or watches a video. Because many children with ASD are visual learners, they latch on to jigs quickly.

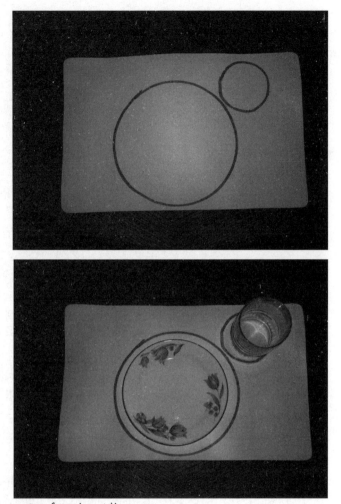

Example of a visual jig

When?

Every bit of simplifying and visually organizing you do in your environment will help your child. So, if you can only take one aspect at a time, that is great! Every little bit helps!

The great thing about these steps is that once you do them, they are done, and the next time you label something or eliminate something, you are just adding to the structure of your home and helping your child to regulate and be more comfortable in his environment.

To learn more

- For shelving cubbies with bins for labeling or without bins, I have found them at low prices on the internet or you can learn to make your own at: www.kaboom. org.

- Plastic bins that are see-through can be purchased at home and garden stores such as Kmart or Target. Plastic colored bins can be purchased online. For colored stacking bins, go to: www.globalindustrial. com.

- To read more about organizing your home for simplicity and clarity, you can access articles for free online at: www.lifeorganizers.com. Just remember to adapt the ideas so that they are simpler and visually clearer.

- Read the novel *Look Me in the Eye* (2007) by John Elder Robison. This gives terrific insight into the behavior and way of seeing the world of young children with Asperger's.

- Many of my ideas for structuring environments visually come from my training with TEACCH in North Carolina. For more information on this fabulous program for people with autism and more helpful ideas, visit their website: www.teacch.com.

Step Five:
Use Music to Help Your Child

Why?

There is just too much scientific evidence showing that music enhances brain development in multiple ways not to use music as a tool! You don't necessarily even have to consider yourself musical as there are multitudes of resources available for use. All people have an innate ability to listen to and use music in multiple ways (Levitin 2006). The right music playing in the background can calm one's entire body, or help it tune in to be more alert. Music inspires your body in an intuitive way to move—and movement is another key to learning. Music is especially helpful to kids with autism because it is primarily a right-brain mechanism, whereas speech and language are primarily left-brained, and that is where kids with ASD have much difficulty. Therefore, music use in repetition can also enhance language development (Springer and Deutsch 2003). Music facilitates spatial skill development too as it helps our brains to see how patterns work and structures time and space. Music is also shown to enhance emotion, and therefore facilitate memory. Music can be motivating and can help to facilitate routines and transitions from activity to activity, or place to place.

Playing an instrument and playing percussion instruments are particularly helpful to a young child's overall development. Playing an instrument and reading music enhances language areas in the brain through different pathways. Hearing music, analyzing it, and modifying one's own sound to fit in with a group, band, or orchestra accesses sections of the brain not often used in other activities. Additionally, playing some instruments requires coordination of both sides of the body and, therefore, the brain (Andreasen 2005). This helps develop motor planning which many kids on the spectrum often have a hard time with.

If you are able to find a teacher who can work with your child to play an instrument or sing in a choir or group, that would be spectacular! If your child is too young right now, keep this in mind for when they reach age five or six.

How?

1. Use the same music at the same time every day to signal a transition or a specific activity. Repetition increases familiarity. Familiarity increases positive response or "liking" of music. Familiarity also helps the child's neurological system to adapt to calming music when used in the same way for the same purpose over time, such as relaxing to eat or to fall asleep. Using the same music for the same activity daily also provides kids on the spectrum with some structure they may not get from language. It may signal what is expected of them, and thereby help guide them in activities.

2. When getting ready to use music to calm, to help alert, or to signal a transition, be sure to think about sound sensitivities. Some children with autism are sensitive to loud sounds; some are sensitive to certain pitches, or certain types of sound—for example, bells or sirens. Some just don't like it when people sing to them! Always start music at low volumes and adjust to your child's reaction.

What and when?

Music that is 60 beats per minute or less is shown to have a naturally calming effect on the human body. You can tap your toe to the beat while looking at the second hand on a watch to see if the beat is slower than, faster than, or matches the speed of the second hand. If that is not going to work for you, see the suggested resources below.

Besides using George Winston's music for sleeping which I mention on page 20, his albums are also useful for calming in general (except for the album entitled *Linus and Lucy*—great music, but use for movement instead of calming). Jim Brickman has much wonderful calming and positive piano music as well. There is something in the fact that these two performers record mainly just the piano. Simplicity with instrumentation seems to help the calming process.

Be sure to start the music as close to the same time for the same purpose daily. For example, if you want to use calming music as part of your bedtime routine, try to play the same piece at 7.30 each night. I suggest playing music for 10–20 minutes for this purpose. If you want to use calming music to help an eating routine, start the same music at the same time every evening a few minutes before sitting down to eat. Playing the music for 10–20 minutes will likely be long enough, but not too long as to overstimulate your child and have the opposite effect.

For alerting music, I suggest *Baroque for Modulation* (TempoSpace Productions) or other pieces by Baroque composers (see *To learn more* below for information). I would play this music daily as part of a routine—either during therapy or tutoring, or during eating or dressing routines. Mozart and Haydn selections are also upbeat and repetitive music for dressing time or other routines.

Pleasant music during the beginning of dinner is also a good strategy to support success at mealtime. As food textures, tastes, and food odors are often alerting to children with autism, calming background music can help them regulate during eating time. Research also suggests that the nerve of the middle ear ends in the tongue, signifying that positive music may enhance taste as well as digestion (Lingerman 1995). Suggested dinner music includes Enya's music, Dean Evenson's work, Lifescapes albums, moving piano music from David Lanz, or light jazz selections.

For interaction, emotion, and language learning, I suggest Hap Palmer's music and the *Wee Sing* collection. Create motions that you can do every time you sing a song together. You can sit at a table while you listen, you can dance within a circle (I like to use hula hoops or stretchy bands to designate visually your circle and my circle), or you can sit together on a bouncy ball, both facing out to look into a mirror. Looking into the mirror helps you monitor your facial expressions and your child can practice hers in a concrete way.

Mirror emotion activity

You can also use music to facilitate specific play with your child. You can use a song to create a play routine and use the natural music pauses to show you places to wait for a child's response or take turns. The old familiar child's song, *B-I-N-G-O* is a good example of this. I also use visuals to represent a song so children can learn to choose a song from the options.

B	shh	shh	shh	shh
I	I	shh	shh	shh
N	N	N	shh	shh
G	G	G	G	shh
O	O	O	O	O

Visuals for the song B—I—N—G—O

Another easy way to create play and language routines with your child is to create "piggyback" songs. A piggyback song is when you take a familiar tune, such as *Twinkle, Twinkle, Little Star* and create new words for the tune. Here is an example of a piggyback song based on that tune for putting on socks and shoes:

Familiar Tune	New Piggyback Lyrics
Twinkle, twinkle, little star	Now it's time for socks and shoes,
How I wonder what you are!	Put them on or sing the blues.
Up above the world so high,	Socks on first to cover toes,
Like a diamond in the sky!	Shoes on next to cover holes.
Twinkle, twinkle, little star	Now it's time for socks and shoes,
How I wonder what you are!	Put them on or sing the blues.

Of course, you may not be putting socks with holes on your children; I threw that in for your amusement. But you get the idea. When you practice creating piggyback songs, you become really good at it!

To learn more

Here are a few books I think you will find enlightening in this area:

- *The Healing Energies of Music* by H.A. Lingerman (1995) published by Quest Books. This book gives you a plethora of lists for the exact music selections for sleeping, eating, alerting, etc. Within this text there is also a thorough list of nature music which is nourishing to the brain.

- *Tune Your Brain: Using Music to Manage Your Mind, Body and Mood* by E. Miles (1997) published by Berkley Books. This book provides wonderful reasons why and how music helps us to focus, heal, relax, and become more creative.

- *Nurturing Your Child with Music* by J.M. Ortiz (1999) published by Beyond Words Publishing. This book provides parents and teachers with lots of ideas and ways to incorporate music into activities for fun, self-esteem development, social interaction, and motor development. This author also provides "music menus" for a variety of purposes.

- To locate CDs by Hap Palmer (*Getting to Know Myself* is my personal favorite for emotional connection games), go to any search engine on the internet and type in "Hap Palmer CD". You can also locate calming music from *Gaiam* and *Lifescapes* in the same way. The *New Age* genre has lots of other choices from which you can select something that you like for calming music.

- Baroque composers include Antonio Vivaldi, Johann Sebastian Bach, George Frederick Handel, and Henry Purcell. Baroque is orderly and repetitive music, and generally is alerting to most children. I encourage you to listen to samples before purchasing to be sure you are getting what you need.

- New music resources for language development, interaction, and emotional sharing come from music therapists entitled *Tuned in to Learning*. They have nine volumes available and include a book and CD. Here is their store website: www.tunedintolearning.com.

- For more children's tunes for songs with gestures, piggyback songs, or language learning songs, go to this really terrific site: www.kididdles.com.

step six:

Create Routines

Why?

Routines provide structure. Kids with autism require structure to help them feel more in control of their environment and know their place in that environment. Routines create predictability. Because language is so confusing to these children, structure also demonstrates visually to a child what is expected of him in any particular place or setting (Quill 1995). Routines can help a child to use time in a meaningful way, to regulate emotionally, and to become engaged with caregivers and teachers. Some children, when left to their own volition, will just run, jump, and squeal for hours on end. Routines help your brain to get ready for daily activities. Routines also help a child with ASD to become independent, while offering parents and caregivers time to do other things besides provide the needed structure for the child. Routines are also helpful if you have other children in the family by providing structure for your child with ASD so you can attend to other things.

Routines are also crucial in helping you learn to play with your child (Greenspan and Wieder undated). A quotation from a friend and colleague's website dedicated to this aspect of teaching and learning with children with autism so eloquently states (Bushey 2009):

> Playing is like breathing, drinking, prayer. Playing is a means of growing attraction between any two souls. If you want a child, any child, to love you, learn from you, imitate you, communicate with you, enjoy you—then play with that child.

(See the *To learn more* section below for details of Tahirih Bushey's website.)

What and how?

The visual schedule to get ready for bed that I described in *Step One* under "Sleeping" is a routine. Using these same parameters, you can create a routine for anything that you have your child do daily.

1. For example, to create a *dressing routine*, take photos of each of your child's belongings as follows: pants, shirt, underwear or pull-up, shoes, and socks. Then place the photos in order, top to bottom with what you want your child to put on first. Use Velcro on the back of the photos and on a folder or piece of tag board to reuse daily. Have your child match the picture to the article, and after putting that piece on, have him put the photo in the "All done" envelope at the bottom of the visual schedule. If you use this every day to teach your child to get dressed, then he will learn the routine of dressing on his own. If your child is too young for this, modify it for just one or two pieces that you know he has the skills to put on by himself—for example, a t-shirt. You can do this with teeth-brushing, using the bathroom, or setting the table as your child gets a bit older.

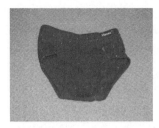

Underwear on

Pants on

Shirt on

Socks on

Visual dressing routine

2. Another routine to create for your child is a *play routine*. This is a simple routine you "play" with your child and his toys, following his lead, but doing some repetitive actions. You can, for instance, create a play routine on the playground. Start out each session with "Let's play on playground!" Go to the swing set and say first, "Let's swing." Swing the child, interacting and pushing for about ten minutes. Then say "Time for slide" and go to the slide. Pick three or four stations and do each activity for ten minutes. Do the same sequence of words and actions each time you go to the playground to teach the routine. You can also use photographs of each playground station to help facilitate this routine.

   This will provide a predictable structure for your child that you can now vary slightly in order to create teachable moments. For an example of a teachable moment, consider the scenario that your playground routine is swing, slide, sandbox, and all done. For a teachable moment after this routine is established, you can intentionally go to the sandbox after the swing. Then you can look at the child, note his reaction, and say "Silly, it's not time for sandbox. It's time for slide!" Here you are teaching flexibility and that it is okay to do something wrong, or out of order. You can't really teach this type of emotional flexibility when there is not a predictable routine in place without causing the child distress.

3. You can also create what is called a *game route*. Using photographs of different play areas in your home and certain toys, you can structure a play routine for your child to learn to do independently. Start simple, so choose four toys that your child loves to play with independently. Then pick four different locations for your child to play in with each toy. Here are some

suggestions: the kitchen table, the corner in the living room, the staircase landing if the child is old enough, a couch or a chair, a rug in another room, a designated spot in the child's bedroom. Take a photo of each of the chosen locations and a photo of each of the selected toys. Then, place one toy in each one of the locations.

Then you want to create a visual game route schedule. On the refrigerator or in some other central place, put the photo of the toys across from the photos of the locations.

Places for game route on the left, toys in that location on the right. Place in the "All done" envelope to indicate moving on to next activity location.

Game route visual example

You have to teach the routine process to the child in order for him eventually to do this route game independently. So, you guide your child to the photos on the refrigerator and say "Time for play" or whatever you would like the cue to be. You say "Look, train—go to rug" while pointing at these two photos. (I encourage parents and teachers to set a timer. This way you can encourage play a bit longer at each station over time.) Set the timer for three minutes. Play with your child in the chair with the train until the timer goes off. Then say "What's next?" and go back to the refrigerator, point to the next location and the next toy, set the timer, and repeat the process. If you stick to the same routine every day for a week, you will be surprised at how much of it your child will be able to do independently.

Variations of this game route include taking the photo of the toy off the fridge and having the child carry it to the chair, match it to the toy, and put it in an envelope at that location. Sometimes, it helps the child to have a matching photo of the toy on the envelope when teaching this process. This is a visual way to show the connection across space in the environment, along with a way to show that the toy in the photo is no longer available when you revisit the schedule on the refrigerator. You can also add an "All done" envelope on the bottom of the game route for the child to be able to see the toy play in that location is done in a concrete way. Some parents have included a favorite video at the end of their game route when originally teaching the routine. This helps some kids with motivation that they otherwise may not have initially. Soon, we hope the play itself becomes the motivator. You can substitute toys or new locations after you have taught the process and your child seems to be engaged with the game route.

Eventually, the child should check the game schedule independently and play until the timer goes off at each station, which then gives parents much needed time to do other things. This also makes a way for others to learn to play with your child and help with supervision when needed.

When?

The easiest way to implement routines is to begin to make a routine out of most activities that you want your child to do daily—such as dressing, going potty, playing, sleeping, bathing—or weekly events—such as going to therapy, Grandma's house, or the store. Start simple, and add when you can.

To learn more

- For ways to structure play routines for all levels of young children with autism, go to Tahirih Bushey's website: www.autismgames.org.

- To learn more about playing interactively with your child within routines, read: Steven E. Gutstein and Rachelle K. Sheely (2002) *Relationship Development Intervention with Young Children: Social and Emotional Development Activities for Asperger Syndrome, Autism, PDD and NLD*. London: Jessica Kingsley Publishers.

- Another comprehensive model for teaching play to children with ASD when you are ready is Greenspan's *DIR/Floortime* found at: www.icdl.com.

step seven:
Take Your Child to Speech/ Language Therapy

Why?

Finding a speech and language therapist is a crucial first step to helping you and your child with autism to experience growth and positive outcomes. Kids with autism spectrum disorders have communication problems that can vary from not communicating with others at all, to echoing others, to talking incessantly. Even children with Asperger's syndrome have communication difficulties because social interaction is communication-based, and the hidden aspects of communication intention and context may be difficult for kids with Asperger's. It may even be that your child talks a lot, but doesn't seem to understand what is told to her. Communication is the foundation of behavior too, so speech/language therapy is very important.

An important thing to know about speech/language therapists is that their training is very intensive and specific. They learn so much about how the brain and body coordinate for speech, language, and subtle aspects of communication that other specialists haven't learned. You will benefit from this expertise on your team of support for you and your child with ASD.

A good speech/language therapist for your child is one who you feel comfortable talking with, and one who seems to connect with your child. Additionally, a good therapist for a child with autism is one who will also *help you to learn how to help your child communicate.* Remember, parents have the most impact on their children's development—92 percent, (Mahoney and MacDonald 2007) while therapists and teachers have 3–4 percent!

This activity not only teaches imitation, turn-taking, joint attention, and language, it also has a sensory hook or pay-off to it.

speech/language pathologist structures play

How?

It would be ideal, of course, if you could find a speech/language therapist who specializes in autism, or who at least has worked with many children with autism! You must ask the therapists you contact specifically about their experience with autism. If the therapists you have access to don't have autism experience, that is okay as long as you get someone who is interested in learning about your child and her differences. What is important is to avoid someone who is not flexible, because we don't ever want the child to be punished for something she can't control. People, even professionals, who don't understand autism may use an intervention that isn't truly helpful if they are not comfortable and familiar with kids on the spectrum.

Positive approach to behavior

This is an example of a behavior from professionals that drives me crazy! I have seen this example so many times of what we *don't* want to happen! A child with autism is hitting in the preschool classroom. So the speech/language therapist and teacher decide to create a visual that says "no hit" and may be accompanied by a symbol. Well, this is a problem first of all because the professionals are assuming the child understands what "no hit" means. Second, this is a negative approach to the issue, and doesn't tell or teach the child *what to do* instead of hitting. And third, this is troublesome because this behavior of hitting is telling us something. The professionals on this child's team should be asking "What is the hitting telling us?" and "What do we need to teach the child to communicate instead?"

"Hands in lap"

What?

Depending on where you live, other names for speech/language therapists may be used, such as speech pathologist, orthophoniste, language therapist, or communication specialist. There are many places you can begin your search for a speech/language therapist. The easiest place to begin is on the internet. Type into a search engine the term "speech therapy" and the name of your country or region in your country. These results will indicate which speech language services may be offered to you. Services may come from private facilities or through regional speech clinics and consultants. You can verify the qualifications of your speech therapist through your professional association for speech language pathology in your country. (See the *To learn more* section below for a link.)

The second place to look for a therapist is at your medical clinic or local hospital. Most facilities have speech/language therapists on staff or have connections to a local clinic they can refer you to. You should also check with your medical insurance and/or other public funding sources to see if this therapy will be covered or if you have to pay for the service out of pocket. This type of therapy is usually more clinical in nature, as opposed to functional, but it is still a critical piece in the "pie" of your child's growth.

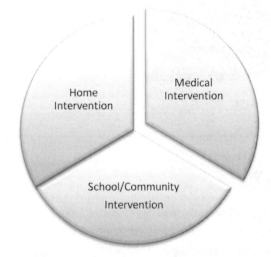

The whole child's growth model

The third place to locate a speech/language therapist for your child with autism is through your local school district. In the US, for example, all children from birth through to age 21 who have a speech/language disability are provided with free education and related service. You can contact your neighborhood school and ask for the early childhood services contact (see Appendix C for more information here). This type of therapy may be home-based while your child is young and the therapist will teach you techniques to use with your child at home. The school district will usually conduct an evaluation of their own even if you have data from other professionals as this is generally required for speech/language therapists in this profession. That is okay because it is another good opportunity for you to learn more about your child's disability and strengths and weaknesses.

When?

Connecting with the speech/language therapist as early as you can after diagnosis is recommended. Early intervention is really critical to helping your child's communication. If your child is only two years of age, that is not too early. Also, some hospitals and clinics may have to put you on a waiting list for services, so it is best to contact them and get on the list if necessary. School settings may be required to serve your child within 90 days of initial request, as in the US, or may have other such timelines depending on where you live. Many families have two sources of speech therapy for their young ones with autism, and although they may be offered in different forms (for instance, at-home therapy and in a clinic), all of the treatment and strategies will be helping your little one tremendously.

To learn more

- Your town may have a university that teaches speech and language therapy to those becoming therapists. If this is the case, the department of speech and language at the university will likely have a clinic and offer services for free or at very little expense. If you live in a town with a university, search its website for "speech and language" or some derivation of that term. If the university has such a department, you will find it in the search results. I generally then choose the "department of speech and language" or the "department of hearing, speech, and language" and that will bring you to the webpage that has the "clinic services" section.

- To learn about what is expected of speech/language therapists who serve children with ASD, go to the website of the professional organization American Speech and Hearing Association—www.asha.org— and type into the search box on the home page "principles for treatment of autism". This site also has a link to international speech/language pathology associations. Type "associations outside the US" into the search box on the home page.

- To learn more about speech therapists and qualifications around the world, go to: www.speech-language-therapy.com/slpworld.htm.

- A terrific parent book to use as resource when you are ready is: *Do-Watch-Listen-Say: Social and Communication Intervention for Children with Autism* by K.A. Quill (2002) published by Brookes Publishing.

- To help you learn how to play with your child while working on language objectives, go to Tahirih Bushey's site: www.autismgames.org. Click on "games collections" and choose from the level and topic of interest.

Step Eight:

Start Educational Services

Why?

There are two main reasons to start educational services for your young child with ASD. The first is because early intervention is critical to long-term success for all children, especially for those with autism. As the brain is very pliable in children under age seven, the sooner multiple services are started, the better the outcome for the child.

The second reason to start education services is because you will gain more perspectives and strategies from people who know autism. Most public schools and programs specifically for kids with autism have professionals experienced with educating children with autism spectrum disorders. These schools and programs can help your child in the areas of socialization, communication, speech, fine and gross motor skills, behavior, and academic or pre-academic readiness skills. Many of these professionals have specific types of training in interventions that really help kids progress in an area. Some interventions you may learn more about in an educational setting include discrete trial, pivotal response therapy, applied behavioral analysis, relationship development, and many others (see the *To learn more* section for links). Some of this training takes years to achieve, and therefore will be extremely valuable to you and your child.

For children and parents living in the US, there is a third reason to begin educational services as soon as possible. The federal law in the United States, Individuals with Disabilities Education Act (IDEA), provides for free and appropriate services to your child based on your child's individual needs (US Department of Education 2004). You need to become familiar with your rights as a parent of a child with a disability under IDEA. This law provides rights for educating your child, that families of children without disabilities don't have, from birth to age 21. This law also challenges you to advocate for your child by knowing the jargon and components of IDEA. For more specifics about IDEA for parents in the US, see Appendix C.

How?

Start with the school in your neighborhood and ask the secretary how to make a "referral for special education testing". Some countries use other terms such as early intervention, early childhood autism services, and exceptional education. I suggest you bring in a dated and signed letter requesting the initial evaluation because then you have a copy of the request in your file.

[Date]

Dear Principal,

I am requesting that my child, [name] be referred for special education testing. My phone number is: [number]. Our address is: [address].

I look forward to hearing from you.

Sincerely,

[Parent]

Sample referral letter for parents to school staff

The school team, called the Individual Education Plan (IEP) team, will notify you to meet within two weeks of receiving the referral (in the US).

At the first meeting, the school team will generally talk about how your child is doing and ask you for input. You will want to share your child's strengths and the things you see he has trouble with. The more examples and details you can provide the team, the better they will be able to determine next steps.

The team should then ask you to give written permission for them to test your child—called an initial evaluation. They will explain the assessment process, and who will test your child. They will also explain if they will come to your house, or if you will bring your child to a school or center for testing. They may also ask you to sign permission to exchange information with your doctors and any other specialist you may have already taken your child to see. This sharing of information is really important because it helps the school team get the best picture of your child's overall needs.

After the testing is completed, the IEP or school team will set up a meeting and invite you to attend. At this meeting, they will discuss what is called eligibility. This is where the team basically asks these two questions, according to *their state regulations*: Does your child have a disability? If yes, does it adversely affect his growth and educational performance? At this meeting, the team members that tested your child will review what they have learned about your child. Don't be afraid to ask the professionals any questions you may have if you are not able to follow what they are talking about, or if they use terms you may not have heard before. There is a lot of jargon at these meetings, and sometimes professionals forget that not everyone is familiar with all of the terms!

The team will then talk through the criteria for eligibility according to their state's interpretation of IDEA or specific criteria determined by the country in which you live. So, for example, they may consider whether or not your child has a *developmental delay* by asking questions such as "Is there a six-months or more delay in speech and language?" or "Is there a delay of six months or more in gross motor skills?" Usually at this meeting they will let you know if they believe your child does qualify for special education services or not.

If your child does not qualify for special services, the IEP or school team will explain your rights to have an independent evaluation (in the US), or provide you with some resources for the areas your child needs support from within your community. If you ask, they have to provide you with a copy of each assessment report and paperwork from the testing process and meetings. Be sure to ask for this, so you will have copies in your file to refer to later on as needed.

If your child does qualify for special education or early intervention services, the IEP or school team will either schedule another meeting with you to draft a service plan, or they will draft one with you at that time. This plan will outline the type of service your child will get and how frequently. The goals for each service provider will also be within this plan, along with the effective dates of the plan. So, for example, your child may qualify for speech/language services and the goal may be "to help [*name of child*] with developmentally appropriate speech sounds", and the service frequency may be two times per week for 30 minutes each. See Appendix B for more samples of educational goals and services.

What?

Your young child may be found eligible for specialized school services, called special education or early intervention, under several different categories, depending on what the testing shows. The most likely categories would be: autism, significantly developmentally delayed, or speech/language impaired. This is where all of the labels your child has gotten become complicated. School systems have different labels than medical systems or certain therapy systems. Please see Appendix C for more help with acronyms and labels.

These services will vary based on your child's age, your child's needs, and where you live. You may have a center in which to bring your child for one-on-one therapy or small group instruction. You may have professionals come into your home to provide service, or you may send your little one to a private or public school. The main thing is to work to get services that you believe help your child to progress in a positive way. If you start a service and don't like it, you may stop it. Some countries, such as the US, are required by law to serve a child with a disability if they are made aware of the child and his needs. Remember that most places have people who want to help you and your child, and will find the best ways to do so.

One of the unforeseen benefits of starting educational services at a young age is that your child will learn to tolerate new environments and to engage with more people. Including school and therapy in your child's routine may spontaneously encourage these skills which sometimes don't come naturally to children with ASD.

When?

Depending on where you live, schools may be required to serve your child starting at age three; other states or countries may require that your child receive early intervention services in some way earlier than age three. Early intervention is internationally a best practice. Most professionals believe that helping kids on the spectrum earlier results in better outcomes. Working with school districts and other programs or institutions may require a lot of energy and perseverance. The nature of public systems does require parents to advocate on behalf of their children. I encourage families to discern when they are ready to do so, and at that point to learn more to be empowered to persevere on behalf of their child's education.

Although early intervention is crucial, not all of the services that schools and institutions offer may be of interest to you initially because, frankly, districts are not required to provide for optimal growth of your child. School districts under federal law in the US, for example, are only required to offer an *equal opportunity to educational access*, not maximize your child's potential (Yell 2005). With children with autism, sending them to a school program for a half or full day may be too stressful, but that really depends on each individual child and the quality of your local programs. If you live in a rural area, you may have fewer services to choose from. Remember, though, that any offer for educational services should be considered in order to support you and your child on this path to learning and growth. Try to come to some agreement on services that work well with your situation.

To learn more

- For parents in the US, only some of your rights involved in this whole process have been mentioned here, with more information provided in Appendix C. To learn about all of your rights when you are ready, go first to: www.wrightslaw.com. This excellent website is written for parents and child advocates and can answer basic and detailed questions about special education law. This site also provides many links and resources for you to expand your knowledge in this area.

- For help in any country, go to: www.autism-india. org/worldorgs.html. This fabulous site has listings of agencies, services, centers, and schools specific to autism by country.

- When you are ready to learn more about your specific state's special education criteria and regulations in the US, go to: www.yellowpagesforkids.com/help/ seas.htm. Select your state's department of education site. Once there, search the site for "special education eligibility definitions". I have success finding the right document with that phrase in most states.

- A very thorough book for parents in this area is *The Everyday Guide to Special Education Law: A Handbook for Parents, Teachers and Other Professionals*, Second Edition (2008) by Randy Chapman.

- For more about your rights as a parent in the US under IDEA, go to: http://idea.ed.gov.

- To learn more about some of the many autism programs and what their basic tenets are, try these sites:

    www.autism-society.org

    www.teacch.com

    www.autismtreatmentcenter.org

    http://education.ucsb.edu/autism/index.html

    www.lovaas.com

    www.icdl.com

    www.rdiconnect.com.

- To learn about some indicators to quality education programs for kids with ASD, see: www.vesid.nysed.gov/specialed/autism/apqi.htm.

step Nine:

Start with the Basic Biomedical Interventions

Why?

For the past several years, there has been an increase in medical research working towards finding a cure for autism. The physicians are learning a tremendous amount about how connected the stomach and intestines are to our brains, and how they vary in a disease-like way in children on the spectrum. The physicians are also learning about interventions that help kids with ASD to grow and become healthier.

Many of these researchers and physicians have learned that there are several contributors to autism spectrum disorders and autistic-like behaviors. Contributors may include pesticides and other chemical exposure, mercury and other metal exposure, preservatives in foods, genetic connections, nutritional deficiencies, medications such as antibiotics, and overexposure to technological devices (Autism Research Institute). We can make good choices about some of these contributing factors in order to help our children (and ourselves) heal.

Biomedical interventions are not a quick fix. Giving a child a supplement is not usually like giving her medication. You won't see behavior changes within a few hours. Biomedical interventions are long-term strategies with big payoff for health, learning, and behavior change in children with autism.

Some families are able to obtain insurance coverage for some of this type of medical support. Some parents pay out of pocket for a nutrition specialist or a homeopathic doctor to help guide them along this path. Some parents just learn what they can and do what they can. Chiropractors often have some naturopathic training as well, so consider them as a possible resource in this area.

I encourage you to begin with a small part of this whole field because I firmly believe that we have to look at the whole child in order to reach success, and also that every little bit helps. This is another area that becomes extremely overwhelming, complicated, and expensive to parents, so just take it one step at a time. Try one or two changes that are manageable for you and see how your child responds to those changes over time. Then you can decide to try more, or stop any interventions you don't believe are helpful.

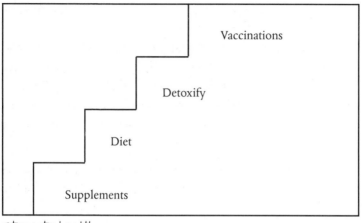

Steps to health

How and what?

First, be sure to notify any teachers, caregivers, grandparents, and babysitters if you are doing one of the interventions outlined below. They need to know for two reasons. First, initially, a child's behavior may get much worse when a change takes place—such as something toxic being eliminated from their diet or environment. This is natural and will improve in time. Second, others need to be sure to follow through with the changes you are making so as to not sabotage the effects. For example, if you are removing all foods with hydrogenated vegetable oils from your child's diet, you must be sure that they have a snack sent in by you for school or daycare, so the child cannot eat something that you haven't been able to screen. And Grandma needs to know so she doesn't, with good intentions, give your child just that which you are working to eliminate!

It is important to teach the other people in your child's life that she is not being punished by a diet or other biomedical change, and not to feel sorry for your child if she doesn't get a cookie or cake when other children do. It is natural to feel this way initially but this really may be just our adult projection on to the child. She is so much better off without that cake that she doesn't feel left out. Besides, there are organic, healthy snack and treat options to add to a child's diet when the need arises. There are many ways to bake these healthy options as well.

1. Supplements to begin with (MacDonald Baker 1997; McCandless 2005; Pangborn and MacDonald Baker 2005; Rogers 2002):

    • Vitamin B6, magnesium, and vitamin C. Research from the Defeat Autism Now work shows that many children on the spectrum do not have enough of these vitamins and minerals in their systems. Also, most foods do not contain enough of these vitamins and minerals to be sufficient, thereby requiring us to take a supplement. These nutrients can help your child's detoxification process which means it helps her to get rid of bad stuff in her body. It also has been shown to have calming effects and increase a child's more neurotypical behavior.

    • Supplement with calcium if you take dairy out of your child's diet. Vitamin D should be added in order to help calcium absorption. Calcium is for more than just strong teeth and bones. It also is responsible for many pathways in our brains and bodies that affect hormones and other body functions.

    • Essential fatty acids are an important supplement to all of us, but especially to children on the spectrum. These nutrients are lacking from our modern diet, and are a natural anti-inflammatory agent. Essential fatty acids are also known to be helpful for many body systems such as immune support, emotional regulation, and skin issues. A favorite no-fillers brand is Nordic Naturals.

- For quality supplements that contain only what you need and no extra fillers, try these brands: Kirkman's Super Nu Thera (very high in vitamin B6), Kirkman's Spectrum Complete, BrainChild's Spectrum Support, Awaken Nutrition, and Nordic Naturals.

- For information on dosage, go to Dr. Rimland's chart: www.kirkmanlabs.com/pdfs/KirkmanBeginnersGuide-Web.pdf.

2. Diet to change (MacDonald Baker 1997; McCandless 2005; Pangborn and MacDonald Baker 2005; Rogers 2002):

- Start by eliminating dairy products (known as casein-free diet) and any foods with dairy in them. Many, many children are allergic to or have a poor tolerance for dairy products. Eliminate dairy foods for two full weeks, and notice any change in behavior, language, sleeping, and eliminating (yes, pooping!). Get any feedback from teachers and other caregivers as well. This will help you confirm if removing dairy from your child's diet was a good start or not.

- Also, as much as possible, buy and eat organic foods. They have no pesticides or hormones and are often richer in needed nutrients.

- Gluten-free diets (wheat-free) are noted to help many children on the spectrum. For some children on the spectrum, gluten acts somewhat like an addictive drug, and therefore, when eliminated, causes significant changes in the child's behavior.

Realistically, these diets are time-consuming to set up and follow through. I recommend you start with the other pieces of this chapter first, and when you are ready and have some support, you take this next step. See *To learn more* below for good resources on this aspect of diet change.

3. Detoxify (MacDonald Baker 1997; McCandless 2005; Pangborn and MacDonald Baker 2005; Rogers 2002):

   • Start by purchasing earth-friendly soaps, toothpaste, and cleansers. There are so many toxic substances in the standard versions of these products that our immune systems are just overwhelmed in trying to eliminate them. Because the immune system of a child with autism is often weakened and because the child is shown to have difficulty eliminating toxins on her own, taking out some of the substances will help decrease the demand on her system. One brand that has been around for a long time is Tom's of Maine, which has soaps, deodorants, and toothpastes without toxic metals or other harming agents. Some good earth-friendly cleanser brands include Seventh Generation and Eco Discoveries.

   • Adding air purifiers to your home is another easy way to help eliminate toxic overloads from your child's system, and your own! House plants help with this process as well.

4. Learn to spread out your child's vaccinations (McCandless 2005; Pangborn and MacDonald Baker 2005). Giving little ones with underdeveloped nervous systems and organs many shots at one time may disturb their development. Several physicians have advice on how to vaccinate your child safely. Try: www.thinktwice. com.

When?

Anytime you can begin one piece of this type of intervention (biomedical), you are helping your child to become healthier. Think of your body or your child's body as a big barrel (Nelson 2006). When the barrel is full, you cannot put any more toxins into it—the barrel will overflow. This could cause the barrel to become damaged. But every supplement you take, every aspect of diet you change, or every way you eliminate toxins from your environment and your body, you are helping the barrel to become less full, and therefore are making your bodies more resilient to the impurities you contact daily. Over time, this helps your child's health and, therefore, her brain; and your child will learn, behave, and grow to be a healthier and happier person. It would be wise, of course, to talk with your physician about biomedical interventions, and, if you can afford it, a nutritionist. Be aware that some physicians may not be familiar with or perhaps do not support the benefits of biomedical interventions. If you get a brush off, do not give up on this valuable and crucial step!

To learn more

- See: www.autism.com. On this site, you will learn from other parents and from the research conducted about the benefits of biomedical interventions, and conferences or references you can read to learn more about them. From this site you can also locate physicians who specialize in the biomedical approach, if you are interested. For an easy start, click on this site's "Families" link and begin with the Frequently Asked Questions section.

- A good resource to help you begin a gluten- and/ or casein-free diet is: www.gfcfdiet.com. This is an awesome and user-friendly website which explains in much more detail why these diets are effective.

- The books *Special Diets for Special Kids*, Volumes 1 and 2, by Lisa Lewis can be found online at Amazon.

- Here is a nice and easy-to-follow summary from the Autism Research Institute if you want to get more involved in further diet changes (such as gluten-/ casein-free) and supplemental options, which includes recommended dosages: http://legacy.autism.com/ treatable/adams_biomed_summary.pdf.

- For more earth-friendly products, go to: www. greenandmore.com or to: www.drugstore.com and click on the "green and natural" section.

- To learn more about the value of essential fatty acids, where to purchase them, and what dosages to use, go to www.nordicnaturals.com and click on the button "Why you should take Omega Oils".

- To read detailed molecular descriptions about toxins and their effects, see Dr. Sidney MacDonald Baker's book *Detoxification and Healing: The Key to Optimal Health* (1997, Keats Publishing, Inc.). This text is very informative, but includes a lot of technical terms. Read this book when you are ready to delve into the biomedical route further.

Step Ten:

Build a Support Team

Why?

I have learned that parents of children with autism often need more support to raise their child than parents of a more neurotypical child. Parenting is the hardest and most important job in our world. Parenting children with ASD makes this job the most stressful, important job in our world. Single parenting only adds more demands to this already challenging work. Teaching children is, in my opinion, the second most important job in our world.

Parents of children with ASD need someone they can trust to teach them about their child; they need someone in the medical field who understands autism to help care for their child; they need educators who are skilled in working with children on the spectrum; they need babysitters and home therapists who understand how to work with their child and allow parents some downtime; they need language and occupational therapists well versed in ASD; and they need friends and family members who will support them and help them with stress and recreation. Other parents get this support network naturally through community establishments such as medical clinics, churches, gyms, schools, and neighborhood recreation centers. It seems that this natural network shrivels up for families with children with ASD as it takes many different strategies to support success in these environments for non-neurotypical kids, and a lot more education!

I think it is important here to discuss guilt. So many parents share that they feel guilty when they even think about taking some time to renew themselves. I think this is natural and should be validated. But I also believe that guilt is wasted energy. Tell yourself that if you don't do some things to maintain your own health and well-being, you won't be available to provide for your child. It is as simple as that. You must build your own activities into the schedule of your family's lifestyle, and learn to include your children in them too.

As the neurotypical child grows, social connections are naturally established. Parents meet other parents whose children are of similar age, doing the same activities, and they become friends and supporters. With parents of children with ASD, they may find this is just the opposite, and the support connections they had previously diminish greatly if not altogether. Many parents tell me that their family friends no longer want to join in activities together because the parents' time is consumed with supervision of the child on the spectrum; others don't know what to do or say. Relatives may be unreliable or afraid to assist with children on the spectrum. Parents of children with ASD have very little downtime to build social relationships and maintain them. That is why I encourage families with children with ASD to actively seek and build this support team. Put it on the list of things to do, just as you would a task of making doctor's appointments or scheduling house maintenance. This is essential to your well-being, and the well-being of your children. Remember that other parents with children with ASD are going to be tremendously helpful and insightful to you. That alone seems to be a common ground upon which support networks can be built.

What and how?

1. As hard as it is to leave your child with someone for an hour or two per week, establish a way to do so and join a parent group (you can help with this through building routines—see *Step Six*). This can be a parent group for autism, or education on autism, or just a support group, but it will be a necessity for your sanity. Sometimes, one parent sits with the child and/or children while the other parent goes to the group and then they come home and share; they also alternate each week so both parents feel connected. You may find a parent group during the day, or an evening group. Depending on your work schedule, where you live, and your other responsibilities, regular attendance at a group of this type will provide you with contact with others "in the same boat".

    You can ask questions about therapies, interventions, schools, programs, etc. You will get others' opinions of what has worked or not with their children. This is not to tell you what to do for your child, but rather to have more knowledge to weigh your options against. Some groups offer childcare assistance during the group time; however, this is often not the norm, so don't have too high expectations. You can even start your own group in your home or in your community if you are willing to advertise that you want to start or host a parent group for parents of young children with autism.

2. Attend as many local workshops, conferences and meetings about autism as you can in the region where you live. Don't be shy to ask for financial help to attend if you need it—many professionals and organizations will discount for parents or exchange the fee for some workshop help. When you are there, make it a point to introduce yourself to as many others as you can and ask if they have children with ASD. These are the parents that you can build relationships with and help to support each other. I see many parents coming together not because they are so much alike, or because they have so many common interests, but because they need each other to help support raising children with ASD.

3. Learn about local Patient Care Assistants (PCAs), respite, and other paid help through your state, insurance company, or Medicaid. PCAs, students, or other assistants can be trained in autism through different agencies as needed. Once you find one or two, you can employ them to help work with your child, play with your child, or babysit your child while you tend to other things, such as social activities and parent groups. You can also find university students who are learning to become teachers and therapists—they can often become wonderful assets to your support team. These students can also be trained to help your child, play with your child, or babysit as needed. You will likely have to pay students out of your pocket.

4. Maintain relationships with the professionals in your child's life whom you have felt were particularly successful with your child. For example, I am still in contact with some young adults with ASD and their families whom I had as students in my classroom as youngsters. These professionals can include teachers, speech therapists, consultants, medical professionals, student helpers, occupational therapists, babysitters, etc. Every now and then, send a note or an email. It doesn't have to be a long or time-consuming communication. Tell the person what is new with your ASD child, and thank them for being part of his life. You can also then rely on these people to be helpful to you over your child's lifespan. You can ask them questions when you are making big decisions, or ask them for their input on something new you are considering. If they cannot comment on something because they feel it isn't ethical, or they are not confident in that area, they will certainly let you know and likely recommend other resources. But we as professionals can and will continue to be a resource for you and your child with ASD because that is our mission and quite typically why we are in the field. I would keep a card file or data file about all of the professionals you take your child to and their contact information. Discard the ones over time that you don't feel made a good connection with you and your child. Maintain the rest.

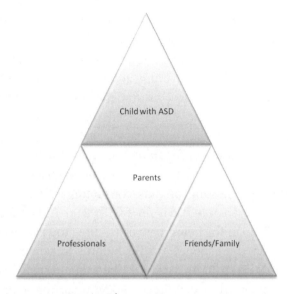

Building a support network

5.　Educate your extended family and your close friends about autism. Most people, I think, shy away from children with these differences because they don't know what to do, how to act, or how to help. You can call official family meetings and share with them what you learn, and what you see helping your child with his behavior. You can also call in professionals to help with this, or ask your family members to attend some therapy or workshops with you. You can't assume because they are family that they will take it upon themselves to learn what they need to in order to help you. Because they may be uncomfortable, they may not feel empowered to do so. Talking about this with them, albeit difficult, is very worthwhile. It may make the difference between keeping a family member in your support network and losing them to visits during once-a-year-family gatherings.

When?

I suggest parents start as soon as possible and build their support group slowly over time. Start with family members, explaining that your child has been diagnosed with autism and what that means. Then discuss with them ways they are willing and able to help. Most families need help in supervision of their child so they can have some time away for their own needs and renewal.

To learn more

- Visit the Autism Society of America's website to locate a parent group (referred to as a chapter) close to your living location. Go to www.autism-society.org and click on "Autism Community" to locate local chapters and international autism organizations.

- Visit the www.yellowpagesforkids.com/help/seas.htm site and type in your state. This will bring up a list of groups, agencies, and programs in your state.

- To locate autism support groups in your region, go to www.childrensdisabilities.info. For online support information, join www.autismfamilyonline.com.

- To learn about worldwide conferences for parent education and to connect with others for support, go to: www.cec.sped.org and click on the "Families" link or the "International" link.

- For current research in the field of autism, go to: www.autism-insar.org and www.autism.com.

Afterword:
You Are on Your Way

In this final chapter, I want to commend you as a person who is committed to helping your own child to be successful and happy; or as one who wants to find ways to work with and educate children with autism spectrum disorders. Parents, therapists, and teachers of children with ASD need constant reminders that although this is one of the toughest jobs on earth, it is ultimately the most worthwhile! When you make progress with one child with autism, you are impacting the future and quality of life not only for that child, but also for many others who touch that life over time.

I hope you have found this book helpful. Its purpose was to provide you with useful, simple strategies to empower you to help your child without the excessive overwhelming facets this diagnosis brings. Each step was meant to stand alone in providing you with the basic understanding of why this step is considered one of the important ten steps to approach with your child. Each step additionally showed you examples of how to tackle the strategy and where to learn more when you are ready. I hope it served these purposes.

Every day, there are new findings in research and new studies of intervention that show success with children with autism. In my journey with these special and unique children, I discount no one's intervention (except for the old Bettleheim (1967) "refrigerator mother" idea!), therapy or treatment. I have learned that maintaining an open mind is what helps us to find the combinations of strategies that fundamentally help each individual make life-changing progress. If an intervention or treatment has not been included here, it is merely because the purpose of this particular book is to help overwhelmed parents and teachers to get started in addressing the needs of these young children. In order to do that, many great and useful interventions are not included, but they are very valuable and worthy of mention over time.

I am sure you are well aware that parents and teachers of neurotypical children don't often need strategies and steps like the ones offered here. Your life is not on that pathway; it is on the exciting and challenging path with very special and unique children. I want to encourage you to continue on the rollercoaster of autism with joy, strength, knowledge, and hope. When you are overwhelmed, take a deep breath and try something new, or try something again. When you are exhausted, take a break, renew yourself, and jump back in again with zest! When you need to know you are not alone, read one of the dozens of books written by parents with a child on the spectrum, or a book written by experts with autism themselves. When you think you aren't doing enough, remember that every little effort you are giving is working. Temple Grandin says in an interview with Tony Attwood that "it was all the little pushes that helped me along the way" (2008). Your efforts will pay off more than you know!

Appendix A:
Sensory Plans

Sensory plan format

Sensory plan information

Target behavior	Setting	Possible function	Time/ frequency
1.			
2.			
3.			

Sensory plan details

Target behavior	Schedule/location	Prevent	Replace
1.			
2.			
3.			

Sensory plan example

Sensory plan information

Target behavior	Setting	Possible function	Time/ frequency
1. Running around room	living room	overstimulated	10.00 and 2.00 daily
2. Only eats two foods	home/school	avoiding texture, smell	daily each meal
3. Gets overexcited when people come over	home	anxiety of new stimuli	only when visitors come

Sensory plan details

Target behavior	Schedule/ location	Prevent	Replace
1. Increase calm state and decrease running around room	9.50 a.m. living room 1.50 p.m. living room	Jump on trampoline for 10 minutes	Wear weighted vest after jumping for 10 minutes
2. Improve eating more foods	11.30 a.m. lunchtime daily home and school	Swing for 10 minutes before eating time	Wear weighted lap blanket while seated for eating
3. Improve calming of anxiousness when visitors come over	10 minutes before visitors are due to arrive	Jump on trampoline for 10 minutes	Sit in rocker with heavy blanket for 10 minutes after visitor has first arrived and greeted child

Appendix B:
Samples of iEP Goals and Services

Service	Amount of time	Location	Service provider
Early childhood services for social and communication development	40-minute sessions, three times per week	In-home services	Early childhood educator
Occupational therapy	30-minute sessions, two times per week	Therapy room, neighborhood school	Occupational therapist
Speech/ language therapy	60-minute sessions, one time per week	In-home services	Speech/ language therapist
Early childhood autism program	Three hours daily, when school is in session	Early childhood autism program, neighborhood school	Special education teacher

Area	Sample goals
Social skills	To improve student's ability to reciprocate interactions with other children of varying ages.
Communication	To increase student's skills in initiating requests and using photos to indicate needs and wants.
Sensory integration	To encourage self-regulation by having the student participate in sensory plan daily.
Fine motor	To help student develop capacity to participate in dressing self, feeding self, and manipulating objects.
Language	To expand student's understanding of language concepts from basic nouns to age-appropriate nouns and verbs.

For excellent help in this area, you can learn about the SCERTS Model at: www.scerts.com.

Appendix C:
Educational Services information in the United States

1. Additional speech/language services

   Check for Scottish Rite Clinics within your area. You can do this via the internet. The Scottish Rite Clinic provides language services to young children, has licensed therapists, and is usually a free service. The other really nice aspect of these clinics is that they generally have a parent education component and that is a unique and important feature. To find out about Scottish Rite Clinics in your area, type "Scottish Rite Clinic" into any search engine, and then within that search type your city and state.

2. Common acronyms in special education

ADA	American with Disabilities Act
ADHD	Attention Deficit Hyperactivity Disorder
ASD	Autism Spectrum Disorder
BIP	Behavior Intervention Plan
DD	Developmentally Delayed

ECSE	Early Childhood Special Education
FAPE	Free and Appropriate Public Education
FBA	Functional Behavioral Assessment
IDEA	Individuals with Disabilities Education Act
IEP	Individualized Education Program
LRE	Least Restrictive Environment
OCR	Office of Civil Rights
OSEP	Office of Special Education Programs
SID	Sensory Integration Disorder
SPD	Sensory Processing Disorder

3. Special education timeline table

- *Initial referral*—This is when parent or teacher asks for testing to be completed in the school; do this in writing. Timeline depends on each individual state's regulations.

- *IEP meeting request*—This is when parent or teacher asks for an IEP meeting to be held to discuss program, objectives, behavior, or other outcomes. Timeline depends on each individual state's regulations.

- *Initial evaluation*—This is the amount of time in which the whole testing process must be completed; parents must give written permission for testing to occur. Within 60 days of receiving parental consent.

- *Complaint response*—This is how long the school district has to contact the parent when a parent files a complaint. Within ten days of receiving the complaint.

- *Due process hearing*—This hearing must be scheduled if LEA has not resolved complaint. Within 30 days of written complaint.

- *Re-evaluation*—Every three years, the child's file must be reviewed, and appropriate testing conducted in order to determine whether or not the child is still eligible for special education services; many districts cut testing, but parents can ask for specific assessments to be conducted.

4. Your rights

   Each state creates their own criteria for answering these questions within federal guidance from IDEA; to find your state's criteria, see the *To learn more* section at the end of *Step Eight*.

These are your rights in a concise summary as the parent of a child with a disability under IDEA in a public school system (private schools don't have to follow these same rights in totality).

First, your child will have to qualify and be deemed "eligible" under the law's categories and criteria. An assessment will be conducted in order for this eligibility to occur. The public school team, called an Individual Education Plan (IEP) team, cannot test your child in any way without your prior permission in writing. Even though you may provide some testing from your physician or therapist, the school district team will still use assessments of their own. This is because they are looking at the educational impact of the autism on your child, not the medical or clinical impact.

The team will have no more than 60 days to complete the testing and hold a meeting, to which you will be invited, to determine eligibility. If they find your child eligible, you will have to give permission in writing for the school personnel to create an IEP and provide services. If they find your child isn't eligible for services based on their assessment, you have the right to ask for an Independent Educational Evaluation to be conducted by a third party at public expense.

If you disagree with the school IEP team, there are multiple ways to address your disagreement. First, you should ask for an IEP team meeting which has to be honored anytime you ask for one, according to IDEA. At this meeting, try to ameliorate your disagreement. Most school teams want to help your child and help you see that her educational needs are being met. If this does not work and you feel your child's needs are still not being met or addressed, you can file a state complaint. Or, you can file a *due process* request which takes your complaint to the highest level of the law. The IEP team will provide you with a copy of these complaint procedures as this is required of them by law. You can also learn more about the complaint process in the resources provided in *Step Eight*.

Bibliography

Amen, D. (2005) *Making a Good Brain Great: The Amen Clinic Program for Achieving and Sustaining Optimal Mental Performance.* New York: Three Rivers Press.

Andreasen, N.C. (2005) *The Creative Brain: The Science of Genius.* New York: Plume.

Autism Research Institute (2009) 'Defeat Autism Now Science Conference proceedings and papers.' Presented at the Defeat Autism Now Conference October 9–11, 2009 in Dallas, TX. Research available at www.autism.com online and at cost for purchase.

Bettleheim, B. (1967) *The Empty Fortress: Infantile Autism and the Birth of the Self.* New York: The Free Press.

Bushey, T. (2009) 'Playing is like breathing.' Available at http://sites.google.com/site/autismgames, accessed on September 8, 2010.

Duboc, B. (2009) *The Brain from Top to Bottom.* Available at http://thebrain.mcgill.ca/flash/index_d.html, accessed on March 10, 2009.

Freed, J. and Parsons, L. (1997) *Right-Brained Children in a Left-Brained World.* New York: Simon and Schuster.

Gomi, T. (2001) *Everyone Poops.* San Diego, CA: Kane/Miller Book Publishers.

Grandin, T. (1995) *Thinking in Pictures.* New York: Vintage Books.

Grandin, T. (2008) *The Way I See It: A Personal Look at Autism and Asperger's.* Arlington, TX: Future Horizons, Inc.

Greenspan, S. and Wieder, S. (undated) 'Developmental, Individual difference, Relationship based (DIR/Floortime) model.' Available at www.icdl.com/dirFloortime/overview/index.shtml, accessed on December 15, 2008.

Levitin, D. (2006) *This is Your Brain on Music: Understanding a Human Obsession.* New York: Penguin Group.

Lingerman, H.A. (1995) *The Healing Energies of Music* (Second Edition). Wheaton, IL: Quest Books.

MacDonald Baker, S. (1997) *Detoxification and Healing: The Key to Optimal Health.* New Canaan, CT: Keats Publishing, Inc.

Mahoney, G. and MacDonald, J.D. (2007) *Autism and Developmental Delays in Young Children.* Austin, TX: Pro-ed, Inc.

McCandless, J. (2005) *Children with Starving Brains: A Medical Treatment Guide for Autism Spectrum Disorder.* Putney, VT: Bramble Books.

Nelson, S. (2006). Personal conversation with this registered nurse on January 18, 2006; she taught me the "barrel" concept.

Pangborn, J. and MacDonald Baker, S. (2005) *Autism: Effective Biomedical Treatments.* San Diego, CA: Autism Research Institute.

Prizant, B.M., Wetherby, A.M., Rubin, E., Laurent, A.C., and Rydell, P. (2006) *The SCERTS Model: A Comprehensive Educational Approach for Children with Autism Spectrum Disorders.* London: Paul H. Brookes.

Quill, K.A. (1995) *Teaching Children with Autism: Strategies to Enhance Communication and Socialization.* New York: Delmar Publishing.

Rogers, S.A. (2002). *Detoxify or Die.* Sarasota, FL: Sand Key Company, Inc.

Robison, J.E. (2007) *Look Me in the Eye: My Life with Asperger's.* New York: Crown Publishers.

Sonnentag, S. (2006) 'Burnout and functioning of the hypothalamus-pituitary-adrenal axis—there are no simple answers.' *Scandinavian Journal of Work, Environment and Health 32,* 5, 333–337.

Springer, S. and Deutsch, G. (2003) *Left Brain, Right Brain: Perspectives from Cognitive Neuroscience* (Fifth Edition). New York: W.H. Freeman and Company.

US Department of Education (2004) *Individuals with Disabilities Education Act.* Available at http://idea.ed.gov, accessed on August 22, 2009.

Yell, M. (2005) *The Law and Special Education* (Second Edition). Columbus, OH: Merrill/Prentice Hall.

Index